Wind Chimes and Promises

◆

To Paul
Blessings!
Love,
Phyllis 5/2002

Wind Chimes and Promises

◆

Phyllis J Adair

Writers Club Press
New York San Jose Lincoln Shanghai

Wind Chimes and Promises
A Memoir

Writers Club Press
an imprint of iUniverse.com, Inc.

For information address:
iUniverse.com, Inc.
5220 S 16th, Ste. 200
Lincoln, NE 68512
www.iuniverse.com

ISBN: 0-595-12529-8

Printed in the United States of America

Dedicated To...

My darling daughter, Karen Coleman-Kelly,
of whom I am immensely proud. I love you so
much. It has all been for you.

Pass the words of this book on to your children.
The next chapters are for you to live and write.
Live them and write them well.

There are few sounds sweeter than the sound of promises kept. The sound
is like wind chimes. If you listen closely, you can hear it.

—Phyllis J. Adair

Contents

Part 3

Part 4

Part 5

List of Illustrations

Foreword

This story of a family told by a daughter in her mother's voice grabs you immediately from the first pages of the flight from Homer, Georgia (Banks County), fleeing the Ku Klux Klan. The family, after several adventures, arrives in Indianapolis to live on a street where their neighbors were Klan.

It is about an immigrant family moving north from Georgia red clay to urban streets, cars and streetcars—a Midwestern city. It is a story of faith, a story of love and what it means to work out the American dream. It is a story about Indianapolis, a city unaware of its prejudices and attachments to the color line or the inequities that fell upon its Black citizens. It is not a race story except that it casually shows how being Black in White America affects you in certain ways. Mostly, you can't do anything about it.

Did it really happen? This is what we want to know. This book is like no other I've read. It is original. It is unique. Every page rings true. You'll meet a grand old Southern lady, a Black man who owned his own farm in Georgia, a white insurance agent with the funny name of Quiggles, hear a real prayer prayed from the depth of the soul, see mature people in love working out problems, enjoy a cameo appearance of Peter Lorre, meet

Uncle Wes who keeps exclaiming "Don't tell me no more!" while all the time demanding all the sordid details.

Phyllis Adair writes a memoir of the life and times of her mother's family that is an important document as well as a beautiful story of a life well lived. I will tell you no more, but invite you to read a book filled with truth, honesty and love, as well as faith and hope.

—**W. Edward Harris**

Preface

Wind Chimes and Promises

is written in the voice of my mother,
Prudence Knox Adair.

All my life, my mother has told me many stories; and
so, I thought I should tell them in her voice. This book
covers fifty of her ninety years, beginning just before
her tenth birthday. I have had the joy of knowing many
of the characters in this book. I loved them so much. I
hope you will too.

Acknowledgements

Thanks To . .

My **parents and family**, and those who have passed on and left such a rich legacy. I am so blessed to have been born into this loving family. If these memories don't exactly match yours, I ask for your understanding, knowing it was all about love.

All my **sisters and brothers**, with whom I am not biologically but spiritually related, for being a part of my life.

Laura Gaus for confidence in my work and me, and for shaking the dust off my mind. Without you, this book would never have been written. I will always be grateful. You are my teacher, mentor and friend.

Bishop T. Garrott Benjamin, Jr. for setting an example for what it takes to bring a vision to fruition.

Rosemary Barringer, a truly unique and exotic rose, for your friendship and typing skills. I am fortunate you came into my life when I needed you most.

AAUW Creative Writers, who listened patiently to the stories, for critiquing and encouraging me. I am so proud to be a part of this group of talented and giving writers.

Crestview Creative Writers, an extension of my family, who kept me grounded and sane.

Jeanne O'Neal who was like a cheerleader and constantly asked: "Is it done yet?" Yes, Jeanne, it is finally done.

You, the reader.

Introduction

Flight from Homer, Georgia (Banks County)

My mother, Prudence, was born in 1909 to William and Sally Knox. She was the fifth child in a family of twelve. All but one of the children were born in Homer, Georgia, but I'm not allowed to simply say Homer, Georgia. I must say Homer, Georgia (Banks County), as if that would explain exactly where it is located. I've never seen it on a map, but from what I've heard, one blink and you're in another county.

The town of Homer, as described to me, consisted of the general store, the post office, the jail and the railroad track, but other than her grandchildren, nothing makes mother's eyes light up like the mention of her home town and her childhood there. It's difficult for me to understand why because it was a hotbed of segregation where she attended a one-room school.

*　　　　　　*　　　　　　*

In 1919, when Prudence was ten, ugliness didn't exist in the eyes of this innocent ten-year-old. She saw only the beauty of the peach trees, the greenery of the woods with its multi-colored wildflowers, the smell of honeysuckle, the whiteness of the cotton fields and the cool, inviting creeks just meant for skinny dipping. After her chores of washing dishes and feeding the chickens and livestock, there was so much fun to be had. There was climbing and stripping persimmon trees, flirting with the boys down the road and tormenting her sisters and brothers. There was always good food, church on Sundays and occasional trips to Miss Abigail's.

Prudence found trips to Miss Abigail's to be a combination of mystery and delight. Miss Abigail was the white lady who lived on the other side of town in a beautiful white house with shutters. Every other month her father, Will, would load up the children, dressed in their Sunday best, for a visit with Miss Abigail. Her mama, Sally, never went and seemed to resent the visit.

Miss Abigail was a tall lady, around 5'8", with gray hair worn in a big bun that practically covered her whole head. She had smoky blue eyes and a friendly smile. She was soft-spoken and hardly ever addressed the children. She patted them and smiled as she sent them into the kitchen for cakes, pies, cookies and milk.

Will often lingered to talk to Miss Abigail alone. After the children had consumed as many goodies as they could, what remained was packed up and sent home with them. Miss Abigail appeared to live alone except for the servants. No one seemed to know anything about her. The children didn't care. They knew she was the source of delectable goodies that they could enjoy, with even some left over to be squirreled away to enjoy for a few days more. Life appeared to be good. Their papa owned a big farm and provided for his family well.

My grandparents were very different in appearance, demeanor and attitude. Grandmother Sally was short, about five feet, dark, with the look of an African princess. Granddaddy Will was tall, about six feet, light-skinned with premature gray hair and smoky blue eyes. Sally never allowed her petite size to stop her. She was an in-your-face, take charge disciplinarian who took no nonsense from her gaggle of kids. She was often heard to say, "I would hock my shimmy for my kids." This meant she would pawn or give up anything she had down to her underwear if her children were in need. Will was gentle and soft-spoken. He often pretended to discipline, but rarely did. He deeply loved Sally and his family. Little did they know then that life was about to change.

A number of rumors began to surface about Ku Klux Klan activity. Before long, rumor became reality and many homes were burned. The chief target of the Klan were black men whom they thought owned property. One night, when Will was in town after dark, he was stopped and threatened by a group of Klansmen, but one of them who recognized him persuaded the others to let him go. After weeks of discussion and preparation, the decision was made to leave the South. Will had relatives in Indianapolis, and a job on the streetcar line awaited him.

Prudence's older sisters and brothers were delighted at the prospect of living in a city. The other children were unconcerned. Prudence had mixed emotions. She was excited about the move because she had never in her ten years been out of Banks County, but leaving her eleven-year-old boyfriend was a little hard to take. The week finally arrived when they were going to take the train to Indianapolis. All the household goods had been sold, along with the livestock.

It was a Tuesday, the summer of 1919, when the children heard the noise of a wagon coming down the road at great speed. Red dust was flying as the horses made their way to their farm. The driver was Miss Abigail, her clothes covered with dust. Her gray hair, which normally sat so perfectly on her head, hung down to her waist and was covered with dust too. She had a broken down shotgun across her lap. She jumped down from the wagon, asked where Will was, then went in to talk to him.

When they finished their conversation, Will told everyone that instead of the end of the week they must leave now. In a flurry of activity, boxes were loaded on Miss Abigail's wagon. With Miss Abigail's help, it took only a few hours until everything and everybody was loaded onto her wagon. During the confusion, Prudence took time to run through the woods to say a hurried good-bye to her boyfriend. Then they were on their way to Gainesville, Georgia to wait for the train.

Will sat in the front, next to Miss Abigail. Everyone kept very quiet. Shortly before they arrived at the railroad station, Prudence noticed a resemblance between her papa and Miss Abigail. Same color hair and eyes and something about the sound of their voices…She thought it was her imagination. The train arrived. The time had come to go. Just before Will got off the wagon, Prudence heard him say to Miss Abigail in a whisper, "Good-bye, Grandmother;" and heard her whisper in return, "Good-bye, Son." After the Knoxes were on board and the train began to move, they looked back for as long as they could to see Miss Abigail, in disarray, sitting on the wagon with the shotgun across her lap.

*   *   *

I have often wondered who was Miss Abigail and why was leaving town so urgent? Was she just a compassionate friend who feared for the lives of the Knox family, or was she my Great, Great Grandmother? Only my Grandparents knew. Some day I'd like to see the town called Homer, Georgia (Banks County). I think when I see that little town, I'll see it as my mother, Prudence, saw it eighty years ago. And, I'll say as I often do: Thanks, Miss Abigail!

"Welcome Lights"

◆

Our few possessions have been unloaded from the wagon and placed on the train. It is almost time to go. Wait! I needed to go to the bathroom, so I slipped away and ran down the railroad track out of the sight of my family. I didn't know I could take care of that on the train. I had barely finished when the train whistle blew. I panicked, thinking I might be left behind. I ran as fast as I could, arriving just in time for the headcount. Present and ready to go are Thurman, Bonnie, Willie Frank (my sister who was named after my father and his brother), Blanche, Boyd, Harold, Bruce, Lois and eight-month-old Ralph asleep in my mother's arms. "Where's Prudence?" someone asked. Whew! I just made it, escaping Mama's wrath again.

We strained as hard as we could for one last look but Miss Abigail could no longer be seen sitting on the wagon with the shotgun across her lap. Whether anyone in the family will ever see her again is doubtful. Homer, Georgia (Banks County) was behind us now and so are our friends and neighbors. I can only imagine the pain Papa must feel leaving the farm he has worked so hard on, to provide for the family. The house we left was our second home. The first had burned to the ground. The cause was unknown, but neighbors and friends, colored and white, helped to rebuild it in a few days.

Mama hated leaving her rose garden. We children often wore the roses to church. How could Mama bear leaving the church graveyard where her first born, Isa, was buried at nine days old? Picking wildflowers to place on her grave had been one of our favorite things to do. My older brother, Thurman, and older sisters, Willie Frank and Bonnie, looked forward to life in the city, life without the chores of the farm and one room schools. They would no longer need to run a mile to use a phone if Mama had another baby or someone was sick.

I had so many thoughts. Would I ever see my best friend, Lucy Tabor, or my boyfriend, Charlie Crane, again? I thought about Grandmother Barnett, my mother's mother, who always helped take care of us when we were sick. Then, there was Grandmother Alice, Papa's mother, who always brought us baskets of goodies. I remembered the time I spent the night with her. I cried all night because I missed my sisters and brothers even though we fought constantly. Poor Grandmother Alice had to walk through the woods to take me home.

I wondered if there would be tornadoes in Indianapolis, because we had one in Homer. All the homes around us were destroyed. Folks said the Knox house didn't blow away because there were so many children holding it down.

Would there be an inside toilet and bathtub? Maybe I would no longer have to share a bath with my younger sister Blanche whom I suspected peed in the bath water. The thought made me mad!

I looked out the train window trying to see as much as I could out of one eye. Just before leaving for the train, my mischievous brother, Boyd, had shot me in the eye with his slingshot. After a few hours, the pain from the slingshot mishap stopped. Mama pulled out a basket loaded with fat buttermilk biscuits and delicious looking sausages that had been gathered up before our hasty departure. We had a feast! We were told we would be living with Aunt Lou for a few days. Aunt Lou is Papa's aunt. Mama was upset about the temporary living arrangements. She said she might need a big stick to keep Aunt Lou out of her business.

It's dark and there is nothing else to see, only the clacking sound of the train can be heard, and an occasional whistle sound as the train nears a city. The motion of the train caused everyone to sleep. Muffled, sleepy voices wake me from my dreams of the woods, the dogwood trees and the pink honeysuckle of Homer. "Look at all the bright lights," someone said. We are approaching Indianapolis. I have never seen so many lights. I am accustomed to the oil lamps at home.

It is the greatest sight I have ever seen. I will never forget these lights that seem to welcome us to our new home.

The time we have waited for has finally come. As I step from the train, I say, "Thank Goodness, finally we're here!"

"Almost Home"

◆

Papa steps from the train carrying sleeping three-year-old Lois. He is followed by my oldest brother, Thurman, who is seventeen and looks just like him. Thurman has hopes for college after his senior year of high school. He is holding tight to slingshot-toting Boyd and mischievous Harold. Wide-eyed Blanche, Willie Frank and I get off next. My oldest sister, Bonnie, is acting in charge and carrying Bruce. Mama gets off last, carrying the youngest child, Ralph, who is still asleep.

Papa is excited and nervous about bringing us to a city we have never seen. He had been to Indianapolis before to visit his brother Frank, Aunt Lou and his cousins. While there, he discussed his decision to leave Homer, Georgia. He had also gone to Chicago, where he had relatives, and made a down payment of $300 on a house there. After coming to Indianapolis, Uncle Frank and Aunt Lou convinced him that Indianapolis was a better place to rear children. He decided they were right but he was unable to get his $300 back from the down payment he had made on the house in Chicago.

He had always dreamed of watching us children grow up on a farm, away from the noise and worldliness of the city. But, it was not to be. He had to continue to provide for his family. He was a farmer and farming was all he knew but, if it took working for the streetcar company or the lumber yard, he would do it. At least they would be away from the boll weevils that attacked the cotton and the Klan who might attack him.

Papa and Thurman went back to the train to unload the rest of the boxes. Then, we waited for Uncle Frank. Papa had called him from the train stop in Tennessee to let him know we were on our way. We, The Georgia Knoxes, waited on long benches in the station. It was nearly midnight.

After an hour, the tired and sleepy children fell asleep; I dozed. We looked like brown and caramel leaves that had fallen perfectly, resting one upon the other. The boys, with the exception of Thurman who is wearing his only suit, wore short pants and shirts. The girls are wearing flannel dresses and underwear of various prints, checks and colors that were well made, without a pattern, by Mama.

Uncle Frank finally arrived and everyone was happy to see him. He had been to Homer many times and had been there a few weeks prior to the trip. Uncle Frank, with little success, tried to teach Lois to say Ind-i-an-apolis, Indiana, but all the three year old managed was, "We are goin' to any apples and bananas."

Uncle Frank had taken the last trolley for the evening to the train station, so we had to wait a few more hours until morning when the first trolley would leave from downtown. After several hours, we boarded the trolley with children and boxes. We are on the way to Aunt Lou's house! I have never seen a trolley; It's trackless and open, with no windows. This is almost as thrilling as the first time I saw an airplane when I was eight years old. On the ride, there is so much to see. The houses are all colors and shapes, and so close together. There are buildings and trees but no woods and streams. After a short ride, Uncle Frank pulls a long cord on the top of the trolley. Nobody understands how the long cord makes the trolley stop. We get off the trolley on a street called Martindale Avenue.

Aunt Lou met us at the door and there were plenty of hugs and kisses. Breakfast is ready and we are ready to devour it. There is bacon, eggs, milk and something Aunt Lou calls donuts. We don't know what they are but we sure like them. There are so many things we've never seen, and so much we need to learn. We have the rest of our lives!

Papa paid Aunt Lou $50 for housing and feeding us for one week, a kingly sum for these days. Mama said that was why Aunt Lou was so anxious for us to stay at her house. It proved to be worth every penny by the time we finished almost destroying the gaslights, and jumping on the furniture. Of course, eight-year-old, rambunctious Harold led the pack. Mama wouldn't allow us to go out much because she felt the street was too busy with the trolley going by, and she was afraid we'd get hurt. So, Aunt Lou's house really took a beating. By the end of the week, Aunt Lou was relieved the Knoxes were leaving and so were we. We were not accustomed to staying indoors. The whole woods had been our playground.

We are moving to our new home, a house owned by Uncle Frank, in a section called Brightwood on the Northeast side of Indianapolis. It is a white, two-story house with a living room, dining room, kitchen, a small room next to the kitchen and three bedrooms upstairs. There is an empty lot on each side of the house, and a big backyard where blueberries, gooseberries, blackberries and rhubarb are growing. It reminds me of Homer, Georgia. Everyone is excited about the new house.

There isn't too much time to be homesick because there is so much to do; school will be starting soon. The rambunctious duo, Boyd and Harold, decided to check out the new neighborhood. It didn't take long for them to discover the ten-year-old white boy, Johnny Snyder, next door. Before they could greet him, he said, "We don't want any little black clouds around here." Harold, not understanding the remark, said, "Me neither." Johnny followed up with, "My father is a member of the KKK." Harold, still not understanding, said, "Mine is too!" The boys did understand that Johnny *did not* want to play with them! They came home and told their older brother and sisters what had happened. They explained what Johnny meant and told them to stay way from the boy next door.

The two Knox boys did what boys sometimes do. When they saw Johnny walking down the alley, they beat him up. Needless to say, my parents were very upset. They did not want trouble in their new home. They had left their Georgia home only to find out the Klan is in Indianapolis too.

"School Days and Mama"

◆

I am ten and it is the first day of school, and I am excited. It has been three months since we left Homer, Georgia. Last night I laid out my best plaid dress. Mama made school clothes for all of us. Papa walked us to school over the weekend so we would know where we were going. I went to bed early, hoping that would make the next day come sooner. We all walked to school together, Bonnie, Willie Frank, Blanche, Harold and Boyd. My oldest brother, Thurman, started to Tech High School. He will be the first in the family to go to a mixed school. It must have been strange for him, as our first day at Public School 37 was for us. Six kids from "the sticks" in the city for the first time, wearing homemade clothes and starting to school was quite a sight.

The day is warm this first day of school in September 1919. The air seems different in the city, thicker and not as fresh as the air in Homer. It's a long way to school, but it gives us a chance to see the sights along the way. We could have gone to the school three blocks away, but there were few colored children there. Mama heard we might not be welcome. She said she wasn't going to allow her children to be subjected to any racial mess. She said she didn't put up with it in the south and she wasn't about to put up with it in the north. She would rather her children walk the eight blocks to school. I don't think Mama knows how cold it gets in Indianapolis.

The school is called a portable school. It is made up of small houses with a big stove in them. There are two classes in each room. All of us were put back a grade. I am supposed to be in the 4A, but I was put in the 4B. I guess they think we are slow because we are from the south. Mama is not pleased. We looked forward to making new friends, but most of the kids ignored us, as if kids from the south are dumb. Sometimes Harold and Boyd fought their way to and from school. Maybe we would have been better off going to the other school. One day Mama kept us at home and went to school herself to talk to the principal. The next day, the teacher announced there had better be no more fights with the Knox kids. And, there weren't! I always wondered what Mama said to the principal. I think Harold misses the fights.

We made it through the first semester. The 4B and 4A were taught in the same room, so it didn't take long for me to learn what the 4A's were being taught. I was skipped a grade the next semester and so were my brothers and sisters.

Winter came and we weren't ready for it. We didn't have snow boots. It got a little cold back home, but not like this. We sometimes had a frost that might ruin some of the cotton. When the cotton was just a bit damaged, it was called crack cotton. Papa would give the damaged bales to us and we would sell them in town. Sometimes we got ten cents for it. I wondered what kids do to make money when they can't sell cotton. The winter got so cold the lot next to our house froze. The boy next door, Johnny Snyder, would skate on the ice. Mama remembered how mean he had been to Harold and Boyd so she went out and poured hot water to melt the ice. She said, "It's my lot." You just don't mess with Mama and her kids. In spite of the cold weather and some unfriendly people, we tried to make the best of it.

Since there are no woods to play in, we spent most of our time on schoolwork. Partly because we didn't have anything else to do, and partly because we wanted to prove to the teachers that we were just as smart, and smarter, than the other kids.

To pass the time, Mama spent a lot of time telling us stories. Some she heard, and some she made up. She is really good at it. When she told ghost stories, we were afraid to go upstairs to bed. One evening, after listening to one of her ghost stories, Blanche and I had to go to the drugstore. When we were on our way home, we saw something white moving toward us across the field. We froze in our tracks. Whatever it was suddenly disappeared. We were terrified and ran screaming home and fell in Mama's arms. We told her we had seen a ghost. She didn't believe us and said we were lying.

A week later, Mr. Lathern, who owned the hatchery down the street, admitted to Mama, when she went to buy eggs, that he saw us coming from the drugstore and decided to scare us. He put on a white sheet and walked toward us. He said he disappeared because he accidentally tripped over a rake and fell down. He was doubled over with laughter when he told it. Mama was not amused and bought no more eggs from Mr. Lathern. She said he probably had a hood that went with that sheet and some kerosene for burning crosses. Mama never did say she was sorry for not believing us.

Most of our white neighbors are friendly, especially the Butterfields across the street who have twin sons. They are nice young men, but Harold said they were sissies. I'm sure Harold would have started a fight with them if he hadn't been nine years old and the Butterfield boys older and stronger. I think Harold is acting out because he is homesick. We all miss our old home, even though we had to share beds, baths and hand-me-down clothes. We promised each other we wouldn't talk about it in front of Mama and Papa because it might make them sad. When I'm alone though, I think about the old house, the fence that lizards sometimes perched on, the tree house, the dolls we made out of sticks, the old mule, the cows that came when I called them, going barefoot and mostly, my best friends, Lucy and Charlie. I think about my grandmothers and Miss Abigail too. I wonder if they miss us. I sure miss them. Mama said you can do anything you put your mind to do, if you want to bad enough. I think

Mama is wrong, but I would never tell her. I think this time she doesn't know what she's talking about. Back home, when I was eight, I read about airplanes and I saw one too! I wanted to fly *really* bad. I climbed up on top of the smokehouse with an umbrella and jumped. I almost broke my fool neck. Mama said it would have served me right. Since I've been in Indianapolis, I've wanted to be back home really bad, and that hasn't happened either. My oldest brother, Thurman, said, "One day you'll be able to think about Homer, Georgia and not be sad." I don't think he knows what he's talking about either. Sometimes, when I close my eyes real tight and lay really still, I can almost taste Miss Abigail's cookies and smell the magnolia back home.

Mama's Prayer

◆

Mama kept me home from school today 'cause I said I was sick but I wasn't. She made me stay in bed. That made me mad, so when she looked in on me, I pretended to be asleep. She tiptoed out and quietly closed the door. After awhile I heard her voice, so I slipped out of bed and put my ear to the door to hear who she was talking to. Mama was praying! I never heard her pray out loud before. This is what I heard:

"Dear Lawd, this is Sal, knee bent and body bowed with my heart in some lonesome valley. I come praisin' you and lovin' you for all you done in my life. You been my leanin' post when I needed somebody to lean on, my walkin' stick when my footsteps got slow, and my feather bed when I needed to lay this tired body down. You blessed me with these ten chillun and a good man, Will, who works so hard. I knows, Lawd, I haven't been as good as I shoulda', but I tried. Folks say my tongue is sometimes too sharp, and they's probably right, but I don't mean no harm. They says I'm too hard on my chillun. When they gits into things, I whup 'em with a strop. Don't the good book say 'spare the rod and spoil the chile?'

I don't 'tend to raise no spoilt chillun. I 'spects 'em to mind. I jest want 'em to grow up to be fine women and men.

I want 'em to have the education I didn't git on account of I got married when I was fifteen. I don't have no regrets 'bout that though 'cause Will is a fine man.

Lawd, I never will forgit the first time I seen Will. I was fourteen and he was twenty. I made it my business to be wherever he was. He was so handsome, tall, fair skinned and curly headed! Everybody said he would never be interested in a gal like me. Didn't they git fooled when Will came one day to ask Mama if'n he could marry up with me.

When we got married and I moved to Will's farm, it was the happiest day of my life. The next year Isa was born. She was a beautiful baby but, Lawd, after nine days she died. Lawd, I'm jest ramblin' on like you don't already know all this. Thank you, Lawd, for easin' some of the pain by givin' me more babies, but there will always be a spot in my heart for little Isa. I knows she's with you, so it's all right. Lawd, I don't ever want to sound ungrateful, 'cause you been too good, but here we are in this strange place and I don't hardly know nobody. The houses are so close together and my chillun don't have no woods to play in. My Mama and family is back in Homer, and my first baby is buried in the churchyard there; and Will misses the farm.

I'm sorry, Lawd, I had to go up to that school house the other day and git them straightened out 'bout them bad kids messin' with my chillun. Lawd, I knows people are right. Sometimes I do speak my mind too much. So, Lawd, I'm asking you to guard my tongue. I would never let

Will and the chillun know how heavy ma heart is, but I can tell you 'cause I knows you won't tell nobody.

Lawd, forgive me for pourin' that hot water on the ice so's that little bad white boy next door couldn't skate on it. I jest couldn't stand him callin' my chillun names; and Lawd, I knows 'bout the chillun sneakin' and puttin' flour and chicken feet on the ol' lady next door's doorstep to torment her. They heard her when she called me a Georgia witch. They know she is a superstitious ol' lady. She say I put a hex on her. Huh, I weren't thinkin' 'bout her. Lawd, you knows I don't know nothin' 'bout that voodoo mess. I'm sorry, Lawd, but it served her right. I thought it was right funny. I knows that ain't right. Vengeance is yours, but I forgits that sometimes.

Lawd, please bless Will and keep him strong. Bless Mama and my sisters back home. I don't want much, Lawd. I jest want my family to be together and happy. Since we been here, the joy has done left my precious chillun's faces. I want to hear 'em laugh again like they used to. I hope they knows how much I love 'em even if I don't tell 'em.

I know in your own time you will answer 'cause you have never failed us. You helped us when the house burned down. You kept us safe through the tornado. You kept the boll weevils from destroyin' all of our cotton, and you kept the Klan from hurtin' Will. I knows you will always see us through.

In Psalms it says 'sorrow may endure for a night but joy comes in the mornin'.' I jest want to know one thing, Lawd, is it almost mornin' yet? It's gettin' so hard to hold on.

This is your servant Sal, A-a-a-men."

I softly said Amen too and quickly jumped back into bed so I wouldn't get caught eavesdropping. I crossed my fingers and hoped God would answer Mama's prayer.

Wind Chimes and Promises

♦

"I'm a teenager now, Hallelujah!" I thought the whole world would change when I turned thirteen. It didn't. I have changed though. My body has taken on a different shape. Mama noticed it right away. She made me wear a bra although I didn't have anything to put in it. Then, she sent me to classes at the YWCA so I could learn all about sex! With as many sisters and brothers as I have, I thought I knew all about it. Boy was I wrong! I tried to find out some things from Bonnie 'cause she's seventeen, but she said, "I didn't need to know." Willie Frank didn't know anything. Mama told me I was growing up and needed to make sure I was always clean. I told her I always do. She said I needed "To wash as far as possible; and to make sure I washed possible too." I said, "Mama, I always check to make sure I smell good!" "Be double, double sure," she cautioned, "Cause if you can smell yourself smelling bad, everyone else is dead." Leave it to Mama. She sure knows how to get her point across. She can be so funny.

I'm doing well in school and getting very good grades, thanks to Mama. She has the ability to remember pages of schoolwork. She doesn't always understand it, but she knows when I'm leaving something out; so she is learning right along with me. I never fake being sick so I can stay at home anymore; so, I don't get to eavesdrop on Mama much except at night. I have to wait until bratty Blanche goes to sleep. We still share a room, and she tells everything she knows. Most of the time Mama and

Papa go to sleep before we do. I guess Papa is tired from working at the streetcar company, and Mama is tired from taking care of us. I *did* get to hear them talking one night 'cause Blanche was asleep. I took my listening position on the floor next to the door. Our room is across from theirs, and sometimes they leave the door open. I heard Papa say:

"Sally, we've been here three years and I still don't like it much. I *don't* like working for the streetcar company. After farming, I'm not used to someone standing over me and telling me what to do. Especially since some people don't treat you with respect. I'm sorry, Sally, I shouldn't burden you with all this. I know things will work out."

"Now, Will, don't you fret yourself. The chillun is doing jest fine; and I'm 'bliged to go wherever you go."

"It's obliged, Sally. You mean you feel obliged to go wherever I go."

"Yeah, yeah. Ain't that what I said?"

"I am glad that you and the children are finally happy. That's the most important thing to me. It's just that it made me feel like less than a man when I couldn't stand up to all those dern inferno Klansmen; and I had to give up the farm to come here. I'm not going to dwell on that. I hope that time will be a healer. You and the children are such a comfort to me."

"I'm glad, Will." (After a few minutes, Mama broke the silence.) "Will, do you 'member when we was livin' in Homer and we went to Commerce, Georgia to shop?"

"Yes, I sure do; we left Bonnie in charge. It was nearing the end of the War, and everybody was jumpin' and shoutin' and wavin' flags. It was a great time wasn't it, Sal?"

"Yeah, it were until we got back. Them dang chillun got into everything. Bonnie had all kinds of reports. She said Harold was so mad we were gone he climbed up on the well and said he was gonna jump in. Bonnie told 'em to go ahead. Thank Gawd he didn't. If that wasn't enough, Thurman told Prudence the end of the world was comin' in a few days. She was out by the smokehouse prayin' at the top of her lungs. She prayed so loud Bonnie said everybody in Banks County and there about heard her."

Mama and Papa laughed heartily.

"Prudence had joined the church and thought she was so holy. She even baptized Harold and Blanche in the creek. She dern near drowned 'em. Course Thurman almost split his sides laughin'. Prudie should have known better than believin' Thurman. She knows what a tease he is. I told Bonnie to make those chillun take their cold pills. When she weren't lookin', they stuck the pills in the cracks of the floorboards. She make 'em dig the pills out and take 'em. That Bonnie is bossy but she gits the job done."

"Sally, your chillun are a real caution."

"My chillun? They gits it from you, Will; and they knows you will let 'em git away with it. They knows not to mess with me 'cause I'll put a strop to they backsides."

"Sally, I have to tell you something." (Papa's voice sounded serious.)

"What is it, Will?"

"Do you remember the time back home when you sent Prudence and Blanche to town to get some thread and it was dark and they had-n't got home?"

"Yeah, Will, I 'members; I told you they was probably playin' around, and when you found 'em to give 'em a good lickin'. Will, did you whup them chillun like I ask you?"

"No, Sally, I didn't. When I found them, they were sleep by the creek. When I woke 'em up, they were so scared. They used the change from the thread to buy some snuff, and they used it. I think it made them sick and drunk. They begged me not to tell you; so I didn't. I thought they had suf-fered enough."

"Oh, Will, them chillun can talk you into anythin'.

"I guess you're right, Sally. I just love 'em too much."

"Lawd, Will, *please* give me a rest from them chillun tonight."

I thought they had gone to sleep, then Mama said sleepily: "Will? Do you 'member that glass wind chime you made me otta broken glass that hung on the porch back home?"

"What in the world made you think of that?"

"I don't know. I guess it was 'cause we was talkin' 'bout the chillun and back home. I loved that wind chime."

"You know, Sally, we had to leave Homer in such a hurry we had to leave a lot of things behind. As soon as I get some time, I promise I'll make you another one."

"I won't be holdin' my breath, Will Knox, but I will be lookin' for it."

"The mornin' will come sooner than we want it to; so, we best get to sleep. Goodnight Sally; I love you."

"Goodnight Will, Gawd bless you. I love you too."

The next thing I heard was Mama hollering: "Blanche! Prudence! What do you have against this door?"

I thought it was Blanche pushing me out of bed like she always did. I had gone to sleep against the door and had been there all night. Mama pushed her way in.

"Git up, gal, and git back in bed."

Little did she know I hadn't been in bed all night. I got up cold and stiff and made my way to the bed. Blanche was sprawled all over the bed like she owned it. I pushed her over and got in. It seemed like five minutes and I heard Mama again.

"Will, don't forgit your lunch bucket. And Will, don't forgit what you promised."

"What did I promise, Sally?"

"Now see, I knowed you forgit— the wind chime, Will!"

I wish they would shut up! I turned over to get a little more sleep. Then that ugly, loud alarm clock with the bells on the top went off. I rolled over and shut it off and tried to go back to sleep. Mama started hollering again.

"Git up, Prudence and Blanche; it's time to git ready for school"

I picked up a shoe and threw it on the floor so Mama would think we were getting up. Then Mama started singing that song she made up from that tired ol' bible verse she says all the time.

"Weepin', weepin' may endure for a night, but joy, Hallelujah, comes in the mornin', in the mornin'."

She sang it over and over. "Well, there ain't no joy comin' to me, Mama," I mumbled. "Be quiet for goodness sakes!" Oh God, there she goes again.

"Don't let me have to come in there with my strop!"

That got my attention; so I crawled out of bed and shook Blanche, who had slept through all of the noise. I don't know why she's so sleepy; she had the whole bed to herself all night. How am I going to make it through the day? I am so-o-o sleepy! I promise, Lord, if you will keep me awake at school today, I will *never, ever* listen at the door again!

He did! So, I didn't!

Papa and the Crying Tree

———— ◆ ————

Papa kept his promise and made the wind chime for Mama. This time Mama made sure it wasn't left hanging on the porch of our home in Brightwood. We moved to a larger house, and the wind chime now hangs on the porch here. I can hear it from my bedroom upstairs. There's a slight breeze, thank goodness! When the wind blows the chime makes a sound like the breaking of thin glass. Sometimes the sound is pleasant and restful. Other times, it's annoying. I don't know why Mama likes it so much. Today it's annoying. I suppose it's because I'm going to another school now, and had to leave my friends behind again. I hated to move, but I must admit I do love this house. It has a large front yard. On each side of the walkway leading to the house, there are big weeping willow trees. In the backyard, we have enough space for a garden. Rhubarb grows by the side of the house and the rosebushes are beautiful. In the living room, the fireplace is trimmed in marble, with wood carved with flowers. Mama' and Papa's bedroom has wooden doors that slide right into the wall! I still share a bedroom with Blanche, and she's still a brat!

I'm upset about a lot of things today; and I don't know who to talk to. Mama just wouldn't understand, and besides, she has a new baby and that keeps her busy. That's why we moved here, we needed more space. It is fun to have a baby in the house again. There was quite a discussion about what to name the baby. After eleven children, it gets harder to think of names.

Dr. Scott, who delivered the baby, wanted to name him "Noble." Bonnie thought it should be "Charles Noble." Thurman, who is the oldest, thought it should be "Omega," in hope that this baby would be the last. Of course, bossy Bonnie won out. The baby is Charles Noble Knox.

The house is quiet today for a change. Thurman has moved to Milwaukee. Bonnie and Willie Frank are visiting friends; the other children are at Aunt Lou's. Only Mama, Papa and baby Charles are here. I'm glad to have some peace. I have a lot on my mind and it all needs to be sorted out. Mama disturbs the peace by yelling up the steps. "Prudence, are you sleep up there?"

"Yes, Ma'am," I lied. "I was just dozing off." I thought that would make her leave me alone. She knew I was mad at her. Bonnie caught me wearing her step-ins. She hollered at me then slapped me. Mama took her side. She had plenty of them, and I would have washed them out. I was so mad at both of them. I thought about running away, but I didn't know where to go. I guess I might as well get up and go downstairs. I'm hungry. I've been up here all day.

I went downstairs to the kitchen to get a glass of milk. Papa came in and asked what was wrong. I told him I had a lot on my mind. He looked concerned and said, "Prudence, how would you like to walk up to the park with me?"

"I would enjoy that," I said enthusiastically.

As we started out the door, Mama yelled, "Will, you can take that corn cob pipe with you. You know you can't smoke it in the house. You oughtta quit smokin' it anyhow."

"Sal, I'll quit smoking my pipe when you quit sneaking around dipping snuff," Papa said with a laugh. Mama didn't answer that.

"Will, if you and Prudie don't get back before supper, I'll be 'bliged to send one of the children after you."

"Sally, you mean you will be obliged to send one of the children after us."

"Ain't that what I said, Will?" Mama knew very well that wasn't what she said. We left her smiling and humming her 'joy in the morning' song.

It was always great to be with Papa; he is always so gentle and understanding. As we approached the park, I said, "Papa, why is Mama so mean?"

Papa looked surprised. "Your Mama isn't mean," he replied. "She is the sweetest woman I know!" I sure can't agree with that, I thought. Papa said, "Your Mama thinks she can beat hell out of you children, and I try to love the hell out of you. Between the both of us, we'll surely get all the hell out of you." He laughed softly. I didn't think it was funny. I know he was trying to make me laugh, but I wasn't in the mood for it.

We got to the park and I spotted a bench.

"Papa, can we sit here?" I asked.

"No," he said, "there's a certain tree I like to sit under; it reminds me of one back home in Homer. I would sit under it when I was troubled." We found Papa's tree and pulled over a bench and sat under it.

"Now, do you want to tell me what's wrong," Papa asked.

"Did Mama tell you about me borrowing Bonnie's step-ins?" I asked curtly.

"Yes," he said. "Suppose, Prudence, that everyone decided they would take things that didn't belong to them. The world would be in a very big mess. Wars have been started because of that very thing."

"I guess you're right," I said reluctantly. Nobody but Bonnie is going to start a war over step-ins, I thought. "That's not all that's bothering me, Papa. Do you remember my friend Margret?" I asked.

"Do you mean the pretty girl they say is half Jewish?"

"Yes, Papa," I replied.

"I've heard quite a few stories about her, Prudence. Some say for sixteen she's pretty wild. Prudence, you've been told more than once to stay away from her. Your teacher even told you, didn't she?"

"I know, Papa, but it's not like people say. She's really a nice girl. I think people are jealous because she's so pretty and talented. I really feel sorry for her, Papa, because her mother left her and she doesn't know where she is; and is not sure who her father is. I heard her father is the Jewish man who owns the grocery store. I do know that he gives her money." Margret is being brought up by her grandmother. An uncle also lives with them. She said the uncle is always touching her and trying to get her to go to bed with him. She's afraid of him!

"That is sad, I can understand her fear and the pain of not knowing for sure who your father is," Papa said sadly. "I only know my father was white, but mother never told us who he was. It was something she wouldn't discuss. My brother, Frank, and I always wondered about it. When I was nine and Frank was seven, mother's sister Anna died. A few years later, Aunt Anna's husband, Sigmond, asked mother to marry him. I think he didn't want to raise his two children by himself. After Sigmond and Mama married, he wasn't always nice to us, and sometimes referred to us as his half-white stepchildren. There were times when he cussed mother and hit her. I would go off into the woods to cry, and pray that things would get better for us. I found a tree in the woods that I called my 'crying tree.' I would sit under it until I felt better. Since coming to Indianapolis, I've found another tree here in the park where I come to think about my problems. I thought you needed to sit under it today. Now, Prudence, you don't need to tell anybody what I've told you."

"Don't worry, Papa, I won't; and nobody will have to worry about me running around with Margret anymore. She left town, and I feel really guilty because I helped her leave."

"What did you have to do with it?" Papa asked.

"Well, Papa, Margret wanted to run away from home and asked me to help her. She wanted to go to New York to be in a dancing group called 'The Brown Skin Models'. She had to slip her clothes out of the house a little at a time so her grandmother wouldn't miss them. I kept the clothes at our house, and I gave her one of those old suitcases we used when we moved here from Homer. Margret said she would call her grandmother later so she wouldn't worry. Papa, please don't tell Mama," I begged.

Papa was quiet for a very long time. Perhaps he was thinking of his own childhood, or maybe about mine. Finally, he said softly, "I won't tell your Mama."

"Thank you, thank you, Papa," I said gratefully. "I didn't mean to do anything wrong. I just felt so sorry for Margret. Nobody else knew how miserable she was. I hope she'll be all right. I miss her so much!" I began to cry, so Papa put his arm around my shoulders. I laid my head against his chest and together we wept under Papa's crying tree.

I didn't know it then, but Mama already knew.

I Learned to Sing

◆

I think there is a lot to be said for spending time under a tree thinking, like Papa does. It's a hot day, so I'm lying under the weeping willow tree in the back yard. I hope no one disturbs me here. When we lived in Homer, there were lots of places to hide and think. I could lay down between the bean poles, or go into the woods. I would daydream and wish I was a boy so I could wear pants. I was such a tomboy then. Boy, have I changed!

My 16th birthday was a few months ago and the earth didn't move. It was pretty much uneventful. Mama did have ice cream and cake for me, but we often have that anyway. I got a few nice gifts—a boy at school gave me a box of handkerchiefs. I really wasn't expecting much.

Papa works only three days a week at the streetcar company; most men were laid off indefinitely. Mama and Papa never complain. I know it must be hard to feed and clothe all of us. They always say, "The Lord will make a way somehow." It appears they are right because we have never been without the necessities, and we are happy.

Thurman is still working in Milwaukee. I miss him! I love the way he teases everybody when he's here, especially Mama. Every time he passes her, he undoes her apron strings. She pretends to be annoyed but she is always happy when he comes home.

Bonnie is going to Indiana University but she had to drop out because money is short. She said she would go back later. She took a job unloading freight from a train. She said it was the only job she could get and it was hard work, and humiliating.

Willie Frank has a job at a fish market. We have eaten so much fish I think we're going to grow fins.

I have been working part time as a clerk at Underwood's Grocery Store. It gives me a chance to get away from home and earn money to buy some of the things Mama and Papa wouldn't consider buying me, like make-up, face cream, and Lily of the Valley toilet water. I told them I needed them; after all, I do date sometimes. Mama said "I didn't need make-up or toilet water, and didn't need to date." I just needed to be clean." I don't even ask anymore; I just can't go through it. I guess she forgot she was married at my age, and I don't have the nerve to remind her.

Life was so much simpler in Homer in many ways. We didn't have to worry about layoffs, food or make-up. When we wanted meat, we went to the smokehouse; for eggs, we went to the henhouse; and chickens were always plentiful. At Christmas, we could go to our property, or anyone else's, and cut down our own Christmas tree. Nobody saw a need for cosmetics. Papa did worry about the Klan sometimes.

I read in the paper a few months ago that a man named D. C. Stephenson is the Grand Dragon of the Indiana Klan; and he's from Georgia too! He was put on trial and given life in prison for the rape and murder of an Indianapolis girl. Maybe that will put an end to the Klan. I sure hope so! I'm going to talk to Papa about that. We always have lively discussions about current events around the dinner table. Perhaps Papa doesn't want to talk about it. I'm sure he must know about it. We spend a lot of time discussing church around the table.

Everybody in the family joined St. John Baptist Church, except me. The church is on our street, seven blocks away. It's just not the church I want to belong to. Everybody tells me I'm going to hell if I don't hurry and make up my mind. I'm just going to take my time. I'll attend there 'til I make a decision. Mama and Papa belonged to different churches in Homer. It didn't matter though because there was the same ol' hungry preacher who would come to town and preach at Mama's church, then Papa's. He would stay at the home of anyone who invited him. Since there were so many children at our house, he couldn't stay with us, thank goodness. He did come to dinner often and I hated it. Mama said the preacher should eat before the children. He always ate the best parts of the chicken; and sometimes, Mama had us fan to make sure there were no flies around the table. I certainly don't miss that. Last Sunday I went to Sunday school at St. John's and talked Mama into letting me miss church. I told her I was tired from working in the store. She knew better but she let me get away with it. I decided to walk home another way. Truthfully, I knew a cute boy lived on the next street over from our house; and I did want to see a church which was also on that street. A friend said I might like it. As I walked down the street, I saw a few boys standing around a truck. As I approached, they started making flirty remarks and whistling. Mama always told me, "When boys act like that, just put your head up in the air and ignore them." She said, "If you talk to them, they will think you're common." Just as I got even with them, the cute boy said, "Hi, Alice;" I said nothing. He said, "Hi, Jane;" I still said nothing. He said, "Hi, Louise;" I just kept walking. He turned to his friends and said, "Uh-uh-uh, ain't that a shame. A good lookin' girl like that, deaf and dumb!" They all slapped their knees and laughed. I had to bite my lip to keep from laughing too. I knew this wouldn't be the last time I saw this wisecracking young man. I found out his name is Morgan Adair and he's very popular with the girls. I told Mama about it. She smiled and cautioned me to beware of smart mouthed boys. If Margret were here, I would talk to her about it. She knows everything about boys.

I got a card from her a few days ago and she said she would be coming back to Indianapolis with the Brown Skin Models. They will be appearing at the Douglass Theater and that's just three blocks away. I'm glad I got to the mailbox before Mama. Now, I've got to figure out how I'm going to see Margret and the show. I've got it! Attucks High School has a basketball game the night of Margret's show. I'll tell Mama I'm going to the basketball game; then, I'll go to Margret's show. There's a problem: I don't want to go alone. I don't want a boy to take me because I'm not sure what kind of show it will be. I think I'll talk Blanche into going. She blabs everything; but if she is involved, she won't be able to tell on me.

"Blanche, I didn't hear you walk up!" (Blanche always likes to sneak up on me.) "When did you get home? How was church? That pink dress looks so pretty on you."

"What are you up to, Prudence? You must want something. Whatever it is, don't ask," Blanche snapped.

"OK, I won't ask," I said. I could see Blanche's curiosity was getting the best of her. I knew she was too nosy to let it go.

"OK, OK," Blanche said. "What is it?"

"Well…" I said, dragging it out as much as I could, "How would you like to go to the Douglass Theater with me?"

"And why, pray tell, would I want to go there?" Blanche said sarcastically.

"Margret will be there with the Brown Skin Models."

"I would love to go but you know Mama would never let us."

"Mama doesn't have to know," I said. "We can tell her we're going to the Attucks basketball game." I could see Blanche was weakening.

"OK," she sighed, "I'll do it; but if Mama finds out, she'll skin us alive."

"She won't find out," I assured her.

"Thanks, Sis, see you later." I leaned back and closed my eyes, feeling very pleased with myself. I mentally finalized my plan, then went in the house to ask Mama if I could go to the game Friday night. Mama said I could go if I took Blanche with me. I told her I would be glad to take her.

The week droned on; I thought Friday would never come. When it did, I was so excited. I hardly slept last night, and I couldn't concentrate in school. Riding home on the bus, I couldn't think of anything other than seeing Margret at the Douglass Theater. I couldn't eat dinner and I told Blanche to hurry up and finish her dinner so we could get dressed to go. We told Mama and Papa good-bye and walked across the street to catch the bus. Blanche was grousing about waiting for the bus since the theater is only three blocks away. She really complained when I told her we were going to get off three blocks past our stop. I told her I didn't want to get there too early. I was afraid someone we knew might see us.

The theater was crowded. The lights were lowered and the show was about to start. The curtain lifted and there were twelve of the most beautiful girls I have ever seen. None of them more beautiful than Margret! The girls wore lovely long satin dresses of various pastel colors. They must have had lots of crinolines under the dresses to make them stand out. They all wore black patent shoes that looked like tap shoes. They sang all of the latest songs, and danced with amazing precision. The show was very tastefully done and there were families with children.

I wonder if Margret's grandmother is here. Maybe if I had asked Mama, she might have let me come. I just couldn't take the chance that she would say No. I wanted to hang around after the show to tell Margret how much I enjoyed the show and how much I missed her. Blanche kept nagging me and saying we better go home.

We left the theater and headed for the streetcar line. I stopped short because I saw a man with his back to us who looked like Papa. When we got closer, I saw it was Papa. He was standing there, smoking his pipe. "Papa, what are you doing here?" I moaned.

"Your Mama asked me to come and walk you home," he said in his usual soft voice.

I thought I was going to faint and broke out in a sweat. I am going to die, I thought. I could picture Mama standing on the porch with the razor strop. I knew it would do no good to plead my case to Papa because he always says, "The one thing I can't abide is a liar." The walk home was one big blur. I could hear Blanche chattering in the background. She was saying it wasn't her fault; it was all my idea. I couldn't even hear the rest. I don't remember much of the three-block walk. Papa wasn't saying anything. A few steps before we got home, I resigned myself to getting the beating of my life. I deserve whatever punishment Mama gives me. To my astonishment, Mama wasn't standing in the yard with the strop in her hand. She had gone to bed! I was totally confused when Papa said, "Goodnight." What on earth is Mama up to? Would she be cruel enough to wait until I went to sleep feeling secure, then wake me and give me a whipping? I didn't fall asleep 'til morning. I woke in a shake with the sun shining brightly. Blanche had already gotten up. I wondered if Mama had already punished her. I waited for Mama to come upstairs, but she didn't. I couldn't stand it any longer so I went downstairs to face Mama. She was on the porch, sitting on the swing under her beloved wind chime, doing the mending.

"Good Morning, Mama," I said sheepishly.

"Good afternoon," she answered.

"Mama, I'm sorry I lied to you about going to the basketball game. I didn't think you would let me go to see..." She interrupted me in mid-sentence and told me to go into the house and get the Bible. She told me to turn to the 13th chapter of I Corinthians. When I found it, she said read it out loud. My voice was really shaky. Mama discussed the chapter, verse by verse. I wondered when she had become so knowledgeable. She ended by telling me how much she loved me and all of her children. She said I should always let my word be my bond and to never degrade myself by lying.

She never told me how she knew I was at the Douglass Theater instead of the basketball game. I wasn't going to press my luck by asking. I thanked Mama and told her I would never lie to her or anyone else again. Mama hugged me, then dismissed me by returning to her mending and starting to sing. I left feeling relieved and happy. Not only because Mama didn't punish me, but because she said she loved me and wanted what was best for me.

I went to the backyard and laid under the weeping willow tree. I can hear Mama singing; her songs are happier now. I found myself singing along with her. I feel I've grown older and a bit wiser today. I thought about everything Mama told me, and about last week's Sunday School lesson. It was about the Israelites who were taken captive by the Babylonians.

The Babylonians wanted the Israelites to sing one of the songs they used to sing in their homeland, but the Israelites hung their harps on the willows and asked, "How can we sing the songs of Zion in a strange land?" Many times I have felt like that. When we left Homer and came here, we hung the harp of our freedom and joy on the willow tree. In spite of all I have endured, I have learned to be happy and, like Mama, I have learned to sing!

The Song Continues

◆

I have heard no more from Margret. I did talk to her grandmother, Mrs. Gibson, though. She said Margret was still with the dance troupe and they were traveling all over the United States. Margret was hopeful that they would go to Europe where Negro entertainers are welcomed and treated royally. She said Margret is starting to make a good living, and plans to send for her soon. Mrs. Gibson is concerned about Margret's safety when she travels; getting a hotel room in any part of the country is almost impossible unless it is rented by the girls who could pass for white. She said most of the time the troupe depended on the hospitality of the local colored people who felt it was an honor to house them. Margret told her the local people welcomed the excitement the dance troupe brought; and many friendships were formed as a result of their stay. Mrs. Gibson said if there were no houses to stay in, the girls would sleep in the manager's bus. It all sounds exciting to me, and I sure hope Margret gets to go to Europe. I would love to hear about all the places I've read about and will probably never see. I asked Mrs. Gibson to be sure to tell Margret that I saw her at the Douglass Theater, and I miss her and know she will be a big star some day! She promised she would tell her.

I will never forget Margret; and I'll never forget the talk I had with Mama the day after Margret's show. I can hardly believe it's been two years since Mama and I had that talk, which I think changed my life for the better. I have changed and so has the lives of the Knoxes. Thurman (the teaser) has moved back to Indianapolis and has married a girl named Georgia. Bonnie and Willie Frank have also gotten married. Bonnie isn't as bossy as she used to be. I think she really misses us since she married. All that quiet at her house must be sweetening up her disposition. I know she really loves us. Sweet Willie Frank, who I used to be jealous of and would torment unmercifully, now lives in Chicago. I must tell her how sorry I am I was so mean to her when we were children. Blanche has a boyfriend, so she's not in my hair much. Harold and Boyd still get into a few fights occasionally; and the other kids are just busy being kids.

According to the paper, the United States is changing too. The country is moving toward a downward economic turn. Jobs are low paying, and practically everybody is buying on credit. The Knoxes are no exception. Papa doesn't like debt; and has always been debt free. If he didn't have the money, he waited until he did. Papa's savings are slowly becoming exhausted and so is he; and no wonder, milk is 21¢, bread is 9¢, and some houses are as high as $8,000. Sometimes he seems a bit morose but he tries to hide it from us.

Papa spends a lot of time in the park under his tree these days. Sometimes he stops by Uncle Wes' house and takes him along. Uncle Wes is Mama's older brother and one of my favorite uncles. He can get on your nerves though. He moved to Indianapolis a few years after we did. Uncle Wes always complains about having a heart condition. Nobody believes he is as sick as he pretends he is. He loves attention; and I think he also suffers from terminal nosiness. He is a lovable old man, and he and Papa get along well. Harold told me that sometimes Papa shares a drink of Uncle Wes' homemade liquor when they go to the park. Harold said he caught them one day smoking their corn cob pipes and having a drink from a Mason jar. He said when they saw him, they hid the jar. I bet Mama doesn't know about that; or maybe she does. I don't know how she manages to know everything. If I had to contend with what Papa does, willful children and a sassy wife, I'm sure I would probably smoke and drink too.

I'm sure I've done my share to cause Papa grief. He was really grieved when I told him I wanted to get married. He cried and Mama became the great interrogator. I have known Morgan for two years but Mama has great reservations about it. Mama and Papa wanted me to go to college, and they both said I was too young. I have no desire to go to college and there's no money for it anyway. I'm working, taking care of a family's invalid mother. I stay at their home during the week and come home on weekends. I think Morgan proposed because he couldn't see me as often as he wanted to because of my job. He also knows about a young man Mama is a lot more impressed with. The young man, Mitchell Brant, visits his aunt across the street. He lives in Kentucky and owns a farm there. When Mama heard he had automatic milkers, she was really impressed. He is several years older than me. He told Mama if he and I married, he would send me to college. I wasn't interested.

I will never forget the evening two years ago that I saw Morgan after the deaf and dumb remark. I was standing in front of the church that I had recently joined. Harold, Boyd and four other boys I just met were standing with me, talking. Morgan sauntered up and said, "six boys and one girl, and I can take her away from all of you." Harold and Boyd probably wished he would; and the other boys couldn't have cared less. What arrogance! I did like his confidence. Morgan always spent more time around the church than he spent in it. Mama knew that as well as some other things. She said she had a friend who knew quite a bit about that Adair boy. She wasn't at all excited about my choice for a husband. Maybe she will change her mind.

I hope I have a marriage like Mama's and Papa's. They have their own private little games; and they know each other so well, they often finish each other's sentences. They are inseparable friends. You can't pit one

against the other. Lord knows I tried; it just doesn't work. It's obvious they love each other deeply.

Mama is planning a family dinner and Morgan is invited. I'm looking forward to all the family being together. Willie Frank and her family will be here from Chicago. Thurman will be here; his wife won't be able to come. Bonnie and her husband, Blanche, Harold, Boyd, Bruce, Lois, Ralph, Charles and, of course, Morgan and myself will be here. We are going to ask Mama and Papa about us getting married. It's been so long since the family has been together. We don't usually have a dinner this big except at Thanksgiving, but Willie Frank wanted to come to Indianapolis while it's still warm.

We have the longest dining room table I have ever seen. Papa made it. There is a chair at each end for Mama and Papa and a long bench on each side to accommodate the whole family. We enjoy sitting at the table together. Sometimes we talk and sing for hours.

All of us girls have been helping Mama cook for days. The dinner is delicious and plentiful. We are having a wonderful time in spite of all the noise the younger children are making. Nobody noticed but me. Mama and Papa didn't seem to be disturbed by it. Bruce is getting a bit obnoxious. When his ball landed in the gravy, that got Mama's attention and was more than she could take! She stood up and demanded, "Will, whip that boy!"

"Sal," Papa said, "He didn't mean to do it, and you know he has a heart condition" (a problem shared by Boyd and the youngest, Charles).

Mama just stood there and gave Papa a dirty look. You could have heard a pin drop. Papa said in an authoritarian voice, "Come here, Bruce, and lay across my lap." Papa whispered something in Bruce's ear, and lifted his large hand to administer the well-deserved whipping. When Papa brought his hand down, he hit his own leg hard. Every time he did, Bruce played along by letting out a yell that could be heard all over the neighborhood.

Thurman could see what was happening and he thought it was really funny. Mama knew what was going on. She wasn't easily fooled. I said, "I don't think it's funny," trying to sound very adult. "Bruce was acting *ugly* and deserved a whipping," I added. Thurman couldn't let that remark go by unchallenged. He said, "Well, I guess you think you're pretty." I should have known better than to take the bait but I said, "Yes, I guess I do." Why didn't I just say no, or not answer at all? Thurman jumped at the chance to say, "Well, Prudie, I think you're pretty ugly, and pretty apt to stay so. Everybody that sees you is pretty apt to say so." Thurman roared with laughter, pleased that I fell into his little trap. I was furious; he had embarrassed me in front of Morgan. I didn't speak to him for the rest of the evening. Everybody was fair game for Thurman that night. Everybody got teased.

Between the good food and the others laughing at Thurman, every one was worn out. Papa decided to take a walk. That meant he wanted to smoke his corn cob pipe. Before Mama could say, "If you aren't back soon, I'll be 'bliged to send one of the children for you," he said he was just going to walk around the block. Bonnie and her husband went home. Willie Frank and her family left to visit other relatives. Morgan and I went to the backyard to sit under the weeping willow tree. We thought we would talk to Mama and Papa after the children went to sleep. All of a sudden we heard Mama screaming. We jumped up and ran into the house. The screams were coming from the front porch. Blanche, Harold and Bruce were standing in front of the screened door with their mouths open, making no sound. Lois, Ralph and Charles were crying. I couldn't believe my eyes. Six-foot Thurman had turned five-foot, petite Mama over his knees and was telling her she had always been a tyrant and he was going to give her a spanking. He was laughing and invited the children to come over and spank her while he held her down. Had he completely lost his mind? This isn't funny. Mama was screaming so loud the neighbors came out and stood on their porches. They were accustomed to hearing noise coming from the Knox house, but they were happy sounds, never anything like this. I didn't know what to do. How could Thurman humiliate Mama like this? Mama started screaming, "Will, Will; Help, Help." I looked up and saw Papa running down the street. He was about a half block away. He was yelling, "I'm coming, Sal." Thurman heard him and let Mama go. He jumped over the banister and started running. There were rocks around the base of the trees and Mama ran out and started throwing rocks at Thurman. And, she hit him with every one. It would have been hilarious if Mama hadn't been so mad. When Papa got to her, she fell in his arms, angry and exhausted. He practically carried her into the house. I thought Mama was going to have a heart attack. Papa was trying to calm her, and he made her lay down. I put the children to bed and tried to explain to them that it was a joke. It will be a long time before Thurman gets back in this house again.

Oh, well, so much for a talk about marriage tonight. I may be wrong, but I thought I saw a smile on Papa's face.

The Name Has A Beautiful Ring

◆

Papa didn't smile for long because Mama was upset with Thurman for a week. She fumed every time she thought about it. Morgan and I thought it best to wait at least a month to broach the subject of marriage again.

We finally got up the nerve, and Mama asked Morgan more questions than a lawyer. You would think Morgan was trying to marry into royalty. Mama has always been a bit uppity. She thinks very highly of herself and her family. She always said her ancestors survived the middle passage from Africa to America and those that survived were the brightest and strongest. I think she is right. When we were in Homer, we had hired-men to help on the farm. I guess Mama felt they did have more than most. I suspect there were three classes in Homer—poor, poorer and poorest; but we were never without anything we needed.

Morgan gained a few points when he told Mama he would bring his mother over to meet her and Papa. When Morgan left, Mama asked, "Is his mother that Indianish lookin' woman who lives down the street from that church you belong to?" I could hear a hint of disdain in Mama's voice because Morgan's mother is Indianish looking, and because I joined a different church than the rest of the family.

"Where did this woman come from anyway and why is her last name different from Morgan's?"

"Well, Mama, I'll tell you. Morgan's mother was born in Rockport, Indiana (Spencer County)."

"Where is Rockport, Indiana, and why did they move here?" Mama asked.

"Morgan told me that Rockport is in Southern Indiana near Evansville in a community they call Little Africa. Rockport is near the Ohio River, across the river from Kentucky. He said he was told that runaway slaves would swim across the river from Kentucky."

"His grandfather had beaten an overseer almost to death because the overseer attacked and raped a member of his family, and he escaped lynching by running through the woods and swimming across the Ohio River to Indiana. It's unknown if he was originally from Kentucky. He changed his last name to Woods and later married Rose Melure. They had twelve children."

"Morgan doesn't know much about his grandmother. Both grandparents had Indian features. Morgan's mother married Henry Adair in Rockport. His father passed away when he was very young and he doesn't remember him. Someone said he was from Adairsville, Georgia."

"What did he die of?"

"Oh, Mama, I didn't ask that. Anyway, his mother later married Mr. Black, who was a widower." I hoped that would answer all of Mama's questions.

Mama bowed her head, thinking over my answers. I could tell she still had more questions.

"Is there anything else you want to know, Mama?"

"Yes, I do as a matter of fact. How many children does she have besides Morgan?"

"She has six altogether: Ivory, Junius, Shirley, Roxie, Charles, and of course, Morgan." Surely Mama doesn't have any more questions.

"Well, I guess I don't have any more questions for now. I'll just wait until I meet her," Mama said. I breathed a sigh of relief. "Oh, one more thing, does Mr. Black have any children?"

"No, he doesn't." I thought I might as well tell her as much as I know. "Mr. Black lived down the street from the Adairs. His wife had been ill for several years. Morgan's sister helped with household duties during her illness. That's how he met Morgan's mother."

"I heard Mr. Black was seeing another woman while his wife was sick. The woman wasn't Mrs. Adair," Mama said, looking smug. "You had better watch Morgan because the apple doesn't fall far from the tree."

"Since Mr. Black isn't Morgan's real father, that doesn't apply, does it, Mama?"

"That doesn't matter," she said.

Could she be right? I hoped not; but unfortunately she usually is. Time will tell.

Then Mama added, "The woman has no lips. It's not natural. Did you say her first name is Mobelia? What an odd name."

Mama can be absolutely exasperating. Poor Papa hadn't said a word; he couldn't get one in. Mama had asked enough for both of them. Thank goodness, she's through for now, I hope.

A few days later, Morgan brought his mother over to meet Mama and Papa. Morgan, with his dark chocolate complexion, does not look much like his mother, except for his high cheekbones and perfect teeth. Mrs. Black has an exotic look. She is a handsome woman. Her brown eyes are narrow, her complexion tawny, her hair, when not braided and pinned in a bun, hangs almost to her waist and is slightly wavy. Her lips are thin. She wears no make-up and had been a member of an apostolic church prior to becoming a Baptist recently. Mrs. Black is a soft-spoken, lovely lady. I could see Mama was charmed by her. Papa is easy and always friendly. You had to work at getting to know Mama.

Mrs. Black talked about Rockport with the same enthusiasm and love that we talked about Homer. She said her family left Rockport because of floods. Many of the men in her family had been a part of a secret society called Sons of Honor that was started in the early 1800s. It was believed they helped runaway slaves, blacks, mulattos and Indians, who crossed the Ohio River.

Mama was intrigued by that. They talked well into the evening about everything, except our marriage. Mrs. Black said she had heard that the Klan was also in Evansville. She talked about all the colored business owners in Rockport, and was proud of her hometown. Clearly, Mama and Papa enjoyed talking with Mrs. Black. It was obvious where Morgan got his charm. They talked on, and on. When are they going to get around to talking about our getting married?

Finally, Papa said, "Mrs. Black, what do you think about Prudence and Morgan getting married?"

"Thanks, Papa," I said under my breath, "at last."

"Well, Mr. Knox, these are hard times; there are so many people out of work. I think things might not get any better. So, I guess there is no reason to ask them to wait until later. Prudence and Morgan can live with Mr. Black and me as long as they wish. We have an extra bedroom."

"That's very nice of you, Mrs. Black," Papa said.

"What do you think about it, Mrs. Knox?"

"I'll think on it for a spell," Mama said.

As far as Mama was concerned, there was nothing else to say on the subject of marriage for now. So, we will wait until Mama thinks on it.

After Mrs. Black left, I had to ask Mama, "What do you have against Morgan?"

"Since you asked," Mama said, "You know Morgan's best friend's family lives across the alley."

"Yes, his best friend is George Turner," I said.

"George's mother told me when George and Morgan were young, she caught them having a peeing contest in the alley."

"So what, Mama, my brothers did that all the time!"

"I don't believe it," Mama said. She was indignant. "Why didn't you tell me; I would have skinned them alive. I won't allow my children to act like heathen."

"I know you would have skinned them alive, Mama; that's why I didn't tell you. That's just something boys do."

Mama looked disgusted. Papa, as usual, had a slight smile.

"Is that all, Mama?"

"No, that's not all. I also heard about a girl named Cynthia Cross, some people called her C.C."

"Yes, Mama; I heard about the neighborhood tramp. People say that C.C. stands for Cootie Crawl," I said with a laugh. Mama didn't laugh.

"I heard that boys line up for her sexual favors," Mama said.

"What's that got to do with anything, Mama?"

"I heard George and Morgan were two of those in line," Mama said.

"Mama, I heard my brothers had been in line too; so, we can't believe everything we hear, can we?"

"Don't you get sassy with me, Miss," Mama said.

"Mama, I'm sorry I asked; can we just drop it for now?"

"Fine by me," Mama said.

I guess I'll keep my mouth shut and just wait.

A month went by, then Mama said she was going to have a dinner. She said to invite Mr. & Mrs. Black, Morgan and the rest of the family. Everyone wondered if Thurman would come because he knows he's in trouble with Mama.

The day before the dinner, we cooked all day. I often wondered where my parents got the money for these big dinners. We had fried chicken, mashed potatoes, mixed greens, candied yams and rhubarb pies. Everything except the chickens were raised by Papa in his garden.

Everyone arrived for dinner. Thurman and Georgia, his wife, were last to arrive. Everyone held their breath, waiting to see what Mama was going to say to Thurman. Thurman and Georgia walked in the door; there was a hush. Mama spoke politely to Georgia; then she said, "Thurman, come with me." Thurman followed Mama, looking sheepish. As Mama closed the door, we heard her say, "As long as you live, don't you ever pull a stunt like that again. I don't care how old you are; I will slap the taste out of your mouth. Do you understand me?" We didn't hear Thurman's answer, the door was closed. Everyone was quiet, wondering what Mama was going to do. The door finally opened and I could tell from the expression on Thurman's face that Mama had given him a tongue lashing. He certainly deserved it. He was lucky to make it out alive.

Papa announced that we should all sit down for dinner. Dinner was delicious. It's always fun to have the whole family at home. After dinner, Mama tapped her glass with her fork and said she had an announcement. She said that she and Papa were giving their permission for me and Morgan to get married. Everyone cheered. Thurman wanted to say something smart but he didn't dare. I was so happy. No more sharing a bedroom with Blanche, baby sitting, and no more Mama telling me what to do. Morgan and I couldn't wait to go to the backyard and sit under the weeping willow tree and discuss our plans to get married. We planned to get married in October. Morgan will continue to work with his stepfather, who has a small construction business and I will continue to take care of the elderly lady whose family I work for.

Morgan decided that we would go to a movie at the Walker Theater with his friend George and his girlfriend to celebrate. The following Saturday was our movie date. Morgan asked me to be ready at 3:00. When he arrived, he, his friend George, and his girlfriend were in a red convertible driven by a man I didn't know. I was so excited; I was hoping the whole neighborhood could see us.

Mama said, "Who's driving that car, Morgan, and where did he get it from?" Mama never minded asking questions.

Morgan said he paid the man to drive us to the Walker Theater, and we would be catching the bus back. Nobody had a car and those that did charged people to take them places to pay their car note.

"Humph," Mama said, "Poor as Job's Turkey and trying to put on airs. Morgan best be saving that money for you to live on instead of squandering it on foolishness."

Papa said, "Have a good time. Don't begrudge the children, Sally."

"Thanks, Papa. Goodbye, Mama." Mama didn't answer.

Riding in the convertible was wonderful; the movie was great, and we didn't mind coming home on the bus at all.

In October we were married in Rev. Mathews wife's beauty shop. She had unexpected guests that we didn't know; so we decided the beauty shop would do just fine. Mr. Black was our witness. Morgan looked dapper in his dark blue suit, white shirt, and blue and white striped tie. I wore a light blue chemise jersey dress with a dropped waist and a bow on the side, with black patent leather shoes. I thought we looked very nice. I was so excited that I heard very little of what Rev. Mathews said. I only heard "to love and to cherish until death us do part." When I said I do, I knew in my heart I always would keep my vows. Finally, Morgan slipped the white gold wedding band on my finger.

At last, I'm Mrs. Morgan Adair. I think the name has a beautiful ring to it.

Some Things Change, Others Don't

◆

After my unceremonious wedding, I went back home to pack my clothes. My happiness had no bounds.

I would never have to wear another one of those asificity (asafoetida) bags Mama makes us wear whenever we have a cold. It doesn't matter how old you are; if you are under her roof, you must be subjected to her roots and herbs. I must admit those bags can cure almost anything if you can stand the smell. I hope Morgan's mother doesn't have any strange home remedies. If so, I guess I'll just have to adjust to them. There are so many adjustments to be made, not only the physical move, but getting used to living in someone else's home.

Morgan's parents' home is a white, single story, frame house. It has a living room, parlor, dining room, kitchen and three bedrooms. The kitchen is one of the largest rooms and accommodates a large table and chairs. Everyone gravitates to the kitchen for coffee and conversation just like we did at home. The house is tastefully furnished with heavy oak furniture. Our bedroom is pleasant. The wallpaper has a pale pink and powder blue stripe against an ivory background. The wallpaper border has tiny pastel flowers. My bedspread is blue chenille. Morgan bought me a blue chenille robe for a wedding gift to match the spread. A small cream-colored chair, with gold-colored wicker inserted in the back, sits in front of a dressing table. The closet is small but it will be adequate for holding my

52

modest wardrobe. It's the nicest room I've ever had; but there is no upstairs. How can people live without an upstairs?

The Blacks have chickens and an old rooster who is so mean he won't let me in the backyard. He chases me and tries to peck me. I won't be sorry if he ends up in the pot. He'll probably be too tough to eat. They also have a large dog. I was told he's a Chinese Chow. He has a beautiful reddish brown coat. I have never seen a dog like him. He is temperamental and doesn't take to strangers. He isn't quite as mean as the rooster.

I'm not used to temperamental animals. All of our animals back in Homer were always friendly. The cows, mules, chickens and even the cat came when you called them. All the animals had special names and seemed to know their names, especially Harvey the cat. I don't know what made me think of ol' Harvey. He died of old age before we left Homer. Maybe after all these years I'm a little homesick for Homer.

I'm glad I'm only two blocks away from home. I can go see the family every day if I wish.

I'm confused about what I should do in someone else's home. I feel like a guest because Mother Black does all of the cooking and cleaning. Sometimes she lets me help but she said she enjoys housework. I can't say I enjoy it but I am used to having chores. I'm not sure I like it but there's not much I can do about it. Morgan said I ought to be happy I don't have to clean anything except our room.

Morgan's mother is more than I could ever hope for in a mother-in-law. She is a sweet, loving woman but she can be over protective about her children, especially Morgan. I hope that doesn't turn into a problem. I would talk to Mama about this but she would only say I should have waited longer to get married. I can't understand why Mama doesn't remember she got married when she was fifteen, or maybe she thinks I don't know. I guess I'll talk to Papa.

I work every day except the weekend so I'm not here to worry about who does the housework. I look forward to weekends for Sunday school and church. I teach Sunday school and really enjoy the children. I have time for walks in the park and visiting the family. I think Morgan gets annoyed because I visit the family so often; but he hasn't said anything yet. It really wouldn't matter if he did.

Neither the Blacks nor the Knoxes have a phone. Harold came over today to tell me Mama wants to see me. He said she wanted to have a family meeting the following evening. I could hardly wait to find out who is in trouble. I know it isn't me, thank God! It surely can't be Thurman again. It probably is Harold who is notorious for getting into mischief; but he was bringing the message, so maybe not. When I arrived at Mama and Papa's house, only Bonnie and Thurman are there. This looks serious. Mama told us her sister Annie is very sick and she must go to Homer to see her.

Aunt Annie's illness could not have come at a worse time. This is 1930 and money is hard to come by. Most people are out of work, and men are selling apples on the street downtown. It didn't seem to phase Mama that there was little money. She said she was going and that was that. Papa said he had saved some money but not quite enough for a round-trip ticket. Thurman, Bonnie and I said we would help. Willie Frank will be told and I know she will mail money from Chicago.

It has been almost eleven years since we left Homer. I can't imagine being away from my brothers and sisters that long; so, I can't blame Mama for being so adamant about going. Our lives have changed dramatically since we left Homer. Thurman, Bonnie, Willie Frank and I are married. Blanche is serious about her boyfriend. Harold and Boyd barely remember Homer. Ralph, Bruce and Lois were too young to remember much; and, Charles hadn't been born.

I wonder where my childhood boyfriend, Charlie, and my best friend, Lucy, are and if they even think of me. I must admit it has been a long time since I thought of them. I must ask Mama to ask about them when she gets to Homer. I closed my eyes and thought how we used to run through the woods, swim in the creek and go to parties where we played a kissing game called Post Office. Mama interrupted my rumination by shouting, "Are you sleep, Pru?"

"No, Mama; of course not."

"This is no time to sleep. I have to get ready for my trip. I'm taking Charles with me," she announced.

"Charles is just five years old. Do you think that's a good idea," Bonnie said. Mama didn't bother to answer because her mind was made up.

We did what we always do; we pulled together as a family to get the money for Mama's trip. Oh how I envied Mama! I would love to see Homer again.

A week later Mama and little Charles were packed and ready to go. The whole family gathered to say good-bye. Uncle Frank, Papa's brother whom we hadn't seen for years, is taking Mama, Charles and Papa to the train station in his old truck. We had seen Uncle Frank only a few times since he met us at the train station when we arrived in Indianapolis from Homer.

Thurman, Bonnie and I promised Papa we would watch the children until he returned from the train station. We spent the time Papa was gone talking about all we remembered about back home. Thurman and Bonnie talked about Aunt Annie, Mama's oldest sister. They spent more time around Aunt Annie than I did. They said they enjoyed hearing Aunt Annie speak a language called Gullah, and said that Mama could speak it too. I have never heard it. I must ask Mama about it when she gets back.

Since there is no one here to stop him, Thurman just had to talk about the time back in Homer when he convinced me the world was coming to the end and I was praying as loud as I could. He laughed until he cried thinking of it, even after all these years. I wish he would pick on Bonnie for a change. He won't because he knows she wouldn't put up with it.

Thank goodness, Uncle Frank just brought Papa back. Papa looks so sad. He and Mama have only been separated once, that's when he came here to find a home for us.

"Well, Sally and little Charles are on their way. I hope they have a good trip," Papa said sadly. It hurt me to see Papa look so pained.

"Mama and little Charles will only be gone for a week or so, Papa," I said. There were tears in his eyes.

"You don't understand, Prudence," he answered.

"What is it I don't understand, Papa," I asked.

Papa asked Thurman, Bonnie and me to sit down. "Do you children know why we left Homer?"

Thurman and Bonnie said they thought it had something to do with the Klan. I was ten years old when we left. I didn't understand about the Klan until much later. I do remember we had separate schools and churches from the whites in Homer. That hasn't changed. We had both white and black friends and neighbors.

Papa interrupted our recollections by saying, "Back then I was warned by my white friend and neighbor, Mr. Patterson, who owned the farm next to ours, that he overheard a Klan member making threats. The Klansman said he and others were going to burn our farm and run us off the land. I didn't take it too seriously. I had heard this kind of threat before. A few days later, I went to visit a friend and stayed later than I should have. It was after dark when I got close to home. Suddenly, I found myself surrounded by about thirty hooded Klansmen. One of the hooded men said, 'Let's string him up!' I'm embarrassed to say I shook all over and was afraid to speak. I thought about the safety of Sally and you children. Not only did I shake because of that, but because I recognized the voices of every man who spoke. These were white men whom I dealt with sometimes on a daily basis. There was the man who owned the store and gave us credit occasionally, and gave you children candy; the blacksmith and the farmer I sold cotton to. The storeowner spoke up and said, 'Why don't we let him go? Will is all right.' I don't know why they agreed; I'm just glad they did. I tried to put the incident behind me." Papa paused. We waited.

"A few days later, Mr. Patterson asked me to ride into town with him to sell some cotton. On the way back home, we decided to stop and do a bit of fishing as we often did. Mr. Patterson was always good to my family," Papa said reflectively. "We got off the wagon, took a short cut and walked toward the creek. We both stopped in our tracks. We couldn't believe our eyes; it was horrible!"

"What was it, Papa?" Thurman asked excitedly.

Papa's hands began to shake but he continued. "We saw a black man, who I didn't know, hanging by his neck from a thick rope on a tree. His hands were tied behind his back. He was shirtless, barefoot, bruised and dead. Neither Mr. Patterson nor I could speak for several minutes. Finally Mr. Patterson said, 'What should we do, Will?' I couldn't answer."

"Maybe we should cut him down," I said.

"We can't, Will. There is nothing to stand on to reach up and cut him down. The wagon is too wide to get down this rarely used path. I think it best, Will, that we get out of here and try to forget we ever saw this."

"I didn't know what to do. How could I ever forget I saw it? I was shocked and grief stricken for this unknown man and his family. It haunts me until this day.

"On the way home, Mr. Patterson begged me to leave Homer for awhile."

"You are like a son to me, I don't want anything to happen to you or your family. I will do everything I can to help you," Mr. Patterson said.

"He did by buying most of our household goods for far more money than they were worth. I have often wondered if Mr. Patterson knew more than he told me. I vowed I would leave Homer and never go back."

"Papa, that was a long time ago; 1919 in fact," Thurman said.

"Unfortunately, not much has changed since then," Papa said.

"I'm so glad we were able to leave safely," Bonnie said in a whisper we could barely hear. She was shocked by the story.

"Why did you tell us this now, Papa," I asked.

"As I said before, some things have changed, some have not. Your Mama hasn't changed. She has a self-confidence that some southern and northern whites might think is arrogance and find irritating. I'm afraid I have encouraged that attitude. I always wanted her to feel good about herself. I tried to instill confidence in you children, too. I love your Mama because she is so small and spunky. Her spunkiness could be her undoing in the South around white people who don't know her. I never told her about all I saw and heard in Homer. I always tried to shield her and you kids from it. I never wanted her to worry. I won't be there to protect your Mama. You know your Mama has a sharp tongue and a short fuse. We must pray for God's protection for her and little Charles," Papa's voice had an urgent plea in it.

We knelt and joined hands. Thurman was visibly shaken by Papa's account of the Klan. Thurman, who was rarely serious about anything, held my hand tightly and prayed earnestly.

Mama is Back

◆

Mama has been gone for almost a week. We miss her so much. I go to see Papa and the kids every evening after I fix dinner for Morgan. Papa has his hands full dealing with Blanche, Harold, Boyd, Bruce, Lois and Ralph; but he doesn't seem to mind. The children are all old enough to be helpful around the house and they are good kids.

Papa can sit on the porch on the wooden swing and smoke his corncob pipe, under Mama's wind chime, without her fussing about his pipe. I think Papa enjoys her fussing. He pays no attention, but he doesn't smoke in the house.

Today everybody is talking about what they think Mama might be doing in Homer. Ralph was a baby when we left Homer. Now, at ten, he has more questions than anyone else. He couldn't believe that when I was his age Blanche, Harold, Boyd and I would go snake hunting in the woods. He thought it was pretty silly; "Nobody with good sense looks for snakes," Ralph said. In retrospect, I must agree.

Papa told everybody Lois was afraid to get on the train when we were leaving Homer to come to Indianapolis. He said she was screaming and kicking and had to be carried. Lois was only three years old and she had never seen a train. None of us, except Papa, had ever ridden on, or seen a train. Lois is thirteen now and not afraid of anything.

The same question was asked everyday: When are Mama and little Charles coming home? Papa gave the same answer: "She'll be home in a few days," he would assure us. He said he had received a letter from Mama saying Aunt Annie was better but was still 'low sick.' I have never been quite sure what that means. I've often wondered if there is a medium sick, or a high sick. Papa said, Mama means Aunt Annie is seriously sick. I'm glad he explained it. I enjoy spending time with Papa. I always feel comfortable asking him any questions, or sharing any problem with him.

Knox Place, as it has come to be called, is simply a warm and loving place to be. The furniture is large and comfortable. The sofas are maroon-colored with large cushions and matching chairs. We have a living room with a fireplace and a parlor, but everybody loves to sit on the carpet in front of the fireplace. As usual, that is where some of us now sit.

"Papa, this is a wonderful house."

"Thank you, Prudence. What made you think of that? Is it because you want a home of your own some day?"

"I would like to have a home of my own, Papa, for a lot of reasons. I've often wondered how you have been able to provide for us so well. I didn't want to pry but I have always been curious."

"Prudence, I was taught at an early age to be frugal, and the importance of learning to read, write and decipher. Those are practically the most important lessons you can learn. Many colored people in the South lost possessions and property because they couldn't manage or save money. Unlearned farmers signed their land away with an 'X.' Some became destitute because they couldn't read, write or do simple addition. That is why I have always made you kids study hard. If you have no knowledge, you have no power over your present or future. Promise me, Prudence, when you have children you will make sure they study hard," Papa said adamantly.

"If I ever have children, I promise, Papa," I said reaching up to hug him from my sitting position on the floor. I didn't ask Papa about the other important lessons. We've probably shared a few of those already. It's time to go home. Harold and Boyd always walk me home even though it is only a block and a half away.

A few days later, Boyd and Bruce came over to tell me Papa received a letter saying Mama definitely would be home Saturday evening. She and little Charles have been gone ten days. I couldn't wait to hear all about Homer. The anticipation of Mama coming home has reduced me to a child again. When I got to the house, Blanche said Uncle Frank had picked Papa up to go to the train station. When Mama, little Charles, Papa, and Uncle Frank got out of the truck, the whole neighborhood knew from the hugging, laughing and shouting that Mama was back home. The neighbors came out and cheered; they, too, loved this little feisty woman who had enough love for everyone. With all she had to do, she was never too busy to be a good neighbor.

We passed little Charles among us, lifting him up and giving him a welcome home hug. He wiped our kisses off. Mama tried to shoo us away and tried to pretend she wasn't glad to see us. She said she was too tired to talk, knowing we were dying to hear every detail, no matter how minute. We all asked questions at once. Mama wouldn't tell us anything until everyone gave her a report on what they had been doing while she was away.

"All right, Mama, you have the family report. Tell us everything about your trip," Thurman said.

"Ask little Charles," Mama said teasing us.

"How was the train ride, Mama?" Bruce asked.

"Peaceful," Mama replied, still keeping us in suspense. "All right! All right! Quiet down, I'll tell you. I see you dern inferno kids aren't going to give me any rest. I must admit I did miss all of you. The last time I had any quiet time was when your Papa and I went to Commerce for a few days. That was in 1918, right after the war. When I got back, you kids had gotten into everything."

"Mama, save us the trip down memory lane and tell us how Aunt Annie is and everything that happened," I said.

"Don't get sassy, Miss. Your Aunt Annie is much better, and the train ride was long and tiring. Little Charles did enjoy the food I packed to eat on the way."

Mama enjoyed telling us about all of the delicious food she took for the trip. She knew how much everyone had missed her cooking. Papa is a good cook but not as good as Mama.

"What did you see from the train, Mama?" Lois asked.

"Not much. Little Charles and I slept most of the way. I had forgotten how long the trip was and how uncomfortable it can be sitting up all the way. When we arrived in Commerce, Georgia, Jeb Tabor met us at the station. It was late, so we spent the night with the Tabors."

"Mama, did you see my friend Lucy Tabor?" I asked. "Lucy was my best friend when I was ten."

"Lucy has moved to Detroit. I think she is going to be a teacher."

Good for Lucy, I thought. My mind went back to all the fun we had back then.

"Mama, what about Charlie Crane?" I asked.

"Who wants to hear about your old boyfriends? You're married anyway," Blanche said.

"Oh, shut up, Blanche," I said.

"If you both don't shut up, I'm not going to tell you anything else," Mama said.

"OK, Mama, but did you hear anything about Charlie?"

Blanche rolled her eyes and looked up at the ceiling.

"I heard Charlie Crane is in the cleaning business and now lives in Kentucky." Mama didn't say he was married. That's what I really wanted to know.

"Do you have any other questions, Prudence?"

"No, Mama; go ahead and tell us what happened."

"Thank you, Missy," Mama said sarcastically. "As I was saying, we spent the night with the Tabors. I sure was happy to get there to get a good nights sleep. We woke the next morning to the smell of fried chicken, biscuits and redeye gravy. It was so good to see the Tabors. They have been good friends. Dorothy Tabor told me her daughter, Luiza, and her family now live on our old farm. I was thrilled to know that I would be able to see our old home again. It was like keeping the farm in the family. Practically everyone we knew years ago has moved north, the Tabors told me."

"Everyone really made over little Charles. They asked about you, Will; and wanted to know how everyone is. They couldn't believe I have four married children. Sometimes, I can't believe it either."

"Anyway, Jeb agreed to drive us to Homer. I was praying his old rusted car would make it. I had forgotten how beautiful the South is. I didn't know how much I missed the pine trees, the dogwood, the honeysuckle and red dirt. It was Sunday and we weren't in a hurry; so, I asked Jeb not to drive too fast because I wanted to enjoy the beauty of the fuchsia colored bushes along the road. I could see at a distance a red truck coming toward us at a high rate of speed. Jeb pulled over."

"That's that wild white boy that's always drunk and starting trouble. Everybody around here knows him and tries to stay out of his way," Jeb said.

"The young man in the truck slowed down and pulled up along side of us. His face was beet red from drinking. 'Whatcha have in there, Jeb; goats?' he asked."

"Why did he say that, Mama?" Ralph asked.

"He was just being nasty and it made me mad. I leaned over and I said, you must be blind and stupid, you redneck fool!"

"Sal," Papa shouted, "You didn't do that. Tell me you didn't do that, Sal." Papa pleaded.

"Yes, I did do that, Will Knox. I won't take that kind of talk from anybody."

Papa shook his head and said, "Lord, have mercy," over and over.

"What else did that man say, Mama?" I asked.

"He asked Jeb what I said, as if I couldn't answer myself. Jeb told him I was just saying the sun was blinding hot. He rattled on, telling him I used to live in Homer and I had moved North; and little Charles and I were visiting my sister who is real sick. I didn't appreciate him tellin' my business."

"The red faced man said, 'Don't you be commin' down here with none of yo' Northern sass. We know how to treat Nigras down here,' as he drove off with his wheels spinning, stirring up dust. I had a lot more I wanted to say. I gave Jeb a piece of my mind."

"We were getting close to our old farm and I couldn't wait to see it. I could see at a distance that a lot of things needed repair. Will, you never would have left the fence unmended like Luiza and her family did. The fence that was left still had honeysuckle covering it. The peach tree was still there. The house looked smaller than I remembered. There were holes in the screen door. Luiza came to the door and I was happy to see her. She fixed lunch for us. It was so strange for someone to fix lunch in a house that used to be ours. I told Luiza we couldn't stay long because I was anxious to see Annie. We sat on the porch for awhile and I had a chance to really look around. It brought back so many memories. The well that Harold stood on and threatened to jump in had been boarded up."

"Why did Harold do that, Mama?" Blanche asked.

"He was mad because me and your Papa had gone to Commerce and left Bonnie in charge. He knew Bonnie would make him behave."

"The smokehouse and the chicken house were still there. Will, as I sat in Luiza's ol' swing, I saw the rusted nail my wind chime used to hang on. I forgot to ask Luiza if she took it down or if it wore out. I did ask her if the Pattersons still lived on the next farm.

"Are the Pattersons still living there, Sally?" Papa asked.

"Mrs. Patterson still lives there. Luiza said ol' man Patterson died a few years ago. Luiza told Mrs. Patterson I was going to be there and Mrs. Patterson asked Luiza to be sure to tell me to come by before I left Homer."

"We left Luiza and headed for Annie's house. I wanted to walk but Jeb said I might lose my way. He said the roads had changed. Annie was sitting on the porch, waiting for us. She said she was so anxious to see me she just couldn't stay in bed. She didn't look well, but seeing us really perked her up. She was surprised to see little Charles. She didn't know I was bringing him. It was so good to see her; it has been ten years since I saw her."

"I know you took charge," Papa said with a smile.

"Of course I did; Annie is my oldest sister and I was determined to get her on her feet before I left. Even with taking care of Annie, I had time to show little Charles the woods. One day I found the old Kings Branch Church I used to belong to. It was boarded up. The school was no longer there. The cemetery next to the church was overgrown with weeds. It broke my heart because that's where my first baby, Isa May, and Mama are buried. We didn't have a headstone for her or Mama but we had placed a large stone to mark the grave. I knew it wouldn't do much good, but I pulled all the weeds around their graves and little Charles and I placed flowers on their graves. I felt I was with my first child, and hopefully, my last one."

Thurman interrupted by saying, "We hope so too."

Mama paid no attention. She just continued her story.

"A few days later, I decided to go to see Mrs. Patterson. I was surprised to see how much she had aged. She was glad to see us but she just couldn't stop talking about you, Will. She said her husband grieved for you for years and said you were like a son to him. She said if you had come back to Homer, her husband wouldn't have died."

"Mr. Patterson was a good man, as good a man as he could afford to be back then," Papa said sadly.

"Well, I noticed ol' lady Patterson didn't say they grieved for me. She probably wouldn't have asked to see me at all if she hadn't wanted to talk about you, Will."

"Aw, Sal, don't be so hard. Don't forget the Pattersons bought most of our things for a good price when we had to leave Homer. If it had not been for Mr. Patterson, we might not have gotten out of Homer safely. There are so many things you don't know, Sal, about how dangerous it can be in the South."

Mama jumped to her feet and put her hands on her hips. She walked over to Papa. Papa is as tall sitting as Mama is standing up. Mama was indignant. She said, "Listen here, Will Knox, I know a lot more than you think I know. Do you think I haven't seen crosses burned and colored men shot? Do you think I didn't know about the man you and ol' man Patterson found hanging in the woods? Do you think I would have left my home, my kin folks, and my baby in that cemetery if I didn't know?"

Papa's face was ashen. His eyes were that smoky gray color they turned when he was upset. We sat on the floor with our mouths open, looking up at Mama. We looked like baby birds waiting for the Mama bird to give us a morsel of food. How did Mama always manage to know everything?

"Why didn't you ever tell me this, Sal?" Papa asked.

"I saw no need. You always know what's best for the family, Will," Mama said softly.

Papa took Mama's small hands in his large ones and said, "Sal, promise me you will never leave again."

"I promise, Will," Mama said.

Mama could calm down as quickly as she could get upset. Poor Papa had tried so hard to protect Mama from what she already knew. We were quiet for a few minutes. I broke the silence by saying, "It's late; I guess it's time for me to go home."

"It's time for all of us to get some rest," Papa said.

"Goodnight everybody; Goodnight Papa. I'm glad you're home, Mama."

"I'm glad to be back home," Mama said with a smile.

By tomorrow, everything will be the same as it was before at Knox Place. At least I hope so.

Tell Me No More

◆
_____

It has been eleven months since Mama went to Homer to take care of Aunt Annie. Unfortunately, Aunt Annie died a few days ago. Mama received the news with grief and resignation. She said she knew when she left her oldest sister that she would never see her again. She was happy she had gone to Homer and spent ten days with her. Her sister, Ivory, and brother, Matthew, who live in Detroit, went to Homer for the funeral. Aunt Annie was the last of our relatives in Homer. I wonder if Aunt Annie will be buried in Kings Branch Cemetery where Grandmother Alice and little Isa May are buried.

Mama knew her brother Wes would not be resigned to the death of their oldest sister. Mama asked Papa to break the bad news to Wes. Papa was the only one in the family who could put up with Uncle Wes' histrionics. No one ever wanted to be the one to tell him any news, bad or good. Papa and Uncle Wes spend a lot of time together since jobs are hard to find. They often go to the park to play checkers and smoke their pipes. Papa agreed to be the bearer of the bad news.

Mama and I were sitting on the porch in the wooden swing when Papa returned from Uncle Wes' house. Papa had his usual smile when he greeted us.

"How did Wes take it, Will? Did he carry on?"

"Carry on doesn't quite describe it, Sal."

"What happened, Papa?"

"I asked Wes to sit down because I had some news to tell him. Wes grabbed his heart and moaned, Oh, Lord, *don't tell me no more!* I hadn't told him anything yet. I told him Annie had passed away."

"Oh, Lord, *don't tell me no more; don't tell me no more.* When did she pass?" He looked like he was going to faint.

"Two days ago," I answered.

"O-o-o, Lord, *don't tell me no more!*" Wes was still holding his heart and leaning back on the davenport. "*Don't tell me no more! Don't tell me no more!* How did you find out?"

"Sal received a telegram."

"Oh, Lord, *Don't tell me no more! Don't tell me no more!*" he continued hoarsely.

"So I thought I wouldn't. There was not much more to tell but Wes, as you know, is so nosy he must know every detail. I think that runs in your family, Sal," Papa chuckled. "Just as I was leaving, again Wes called out, 'Will, *don't tell me no more*; but is Ivory and Matt going to the funeral?' I told him they were."

"It has been so long since I've been to Homer and I sure miss it, Will."
"Wes continued to clutch his heart and hold his head. I know Wes well enough to know when he is all right. I gave him a drink of water and headed for the door. When I got to the porch, Wes yelled out, 'Will, *don't tell me no more.* How is Sally taking it?' I told him you were holding on. I hurried home before he could think of anything else I shouldn't tell him."

"Papa, weren't you afraid Uncle Wes might have a heart attack?"

Before Papa could answer, Mama said, "Aw pshaw, Wes has been having a heart attack for the last twenty years. He can be a real vexation. He'll outlive us all."

We smiled, thinking about Uncle Wes' antics. "He will never change," Mama said.

Papa left us and went to the backyard to work in his garden. I wanted to tell Mama I'm pregnant but after all that has happened, this isn't a good time.

"Mama, you never did tell me if you found out if Charlie Crane is married."

"Charlie Crane again, huh? Yes, he is married. Why do you want to know?"

"I was just curious."

"I had other things to think about. After I took care of Annie each day, I had time to walk through the woods and see the colorful wild flowers. I sat on the creek bank and dangled my feet in the cool water. Of course, I kept a stick near by in case of snakes. The butterflies during the day and the fireflies at night are far more beautiful and plentiful than they are in Indianapolis. Me and Little Charles went back to the cemetery several times. I had time to think. I have precious little time to do that around here."

"Those dern green lizards in Homer still drive me crazy. I remember when I was sick with that flu the soldiers brought back from the war. Everybody was dying so fast they were buried in mass graves. When I was lying in bed, praying I wouldn't die and leave all you children, those dern lizards were sitting on the fence like they were waiting for me to die. That's why I hate them. I'm glad there are no lizards in Indianapolis."

"I went back to see Luiza again. I just had to see our old farm once more before I left. As I walked to the back of the house, I remembered old Harvey the cat. Do you remember Harvey, Pru?" Mama didn't wait for my answer. "I do remember old Harvey was Thurman's cat and we had him for years. Thurman really loved him. Well, Harvey got sick and looked like he was suffering. Your Papa decided it was time to put him out of his misery. Thurman was heartbroken and cried. That was unusual for him. Thurman said Harvey had always played with you children and was an expert mouse catcher. Your Papa had gotten his shotgun and started down the road with old Harvey. Thurman was beside himself with grief, but I thought ending Harvey's misery was the right thing to do. Thurman said, 'Mama, when you get old, I will never think of taking you out and shooting you.' Run fast and get your Papa, boy," I said, "And tell him to bring old Harvey back home. Thurman caught up with your Papa and brought Harvey back home where he died peacefully in his sleep two weeks later. We buried Harvey in the backyard. The big stone you children placed on Harvey's grave was still there."

"So many memories came back to me when I went back into the house and walked into our bedroom. I remembered when I was in labor with Harold. Your Papa thought I was going to have a hard time so he went to get the doctor, who was white and the only doctor in town. He would treat colored folks as long as no one knew about it. So, the whites pretended they didn't know. The doctor had been at the house for hours and I was still in labor. He had been up all night and was tired, so he climbed over me to the other side of the bed and went to sleep. When your Papa came in and saw the doctor in bed with me, asleep, I thought he would burst his sides laughing. 'I sure wish we had a picture of that,' he said." Mama laughed and slapped her knee. She kept on talking as if I wasn't there. "Your Papa teased me by saying Harold looked more like the doctor than him."

"It was sure good to be back home, except I missed all of our friends that used to live in Homer. I decided this would be the last time I would visit Luiza and her family on our old farm. There were just too many memories. I called little Charles in from play and told him it was time to go. As we walked back to Annie's, I saw the clearing where all of our friends and family would gather for our yearly barbecue, pig roast and fish fry. People would come from Commerce, Gainesville, and some even came from Macon. The ladies brought pies, cakes, jellies, jams and all sorts of home made food they had canned. They showed off the quilts they had been working on and bragged about their children. The men pitched horseshoes and talked about their crops and lied about how big the fish were they caught. We looked forward to this every year. The picnic took place every year at the same time."

"All of our friends and family had to pass by the Johnson farm. This was the white family who lived next to the Pattersons. Every year, ol' lady Johnson would ask me the same question. When she saw us on the wagon, she would stand on her porch and holler, 'Who died, Sally?' Dern nosy woman always wanted to know colored folk's business. Made me mad, so I would holler back, I don't know who all. Every year she would just say, 'Oh,' and go back and sit down on the porch. I did like that ol' lady even though she was nosy. I guess she's probably dead now."

"It was so good to hear that slow Georgia drawl again and to move slower than we do here; but I am glad to be back home because this is my home now."

I don't recall Mama ever being so talkative. "Mama, did you see Miss Abigail when you were back home?" I asked.

"No, Annie said she passed away a long time ago."

"Mama, who was Miss Abigail? Do you know anything about her?"

"No," Mama said, then got up abruptly. "Let's go into the house, Prudence."

I followed Mama into the house and we went into the kitchen and sat down at the table. Mama took buttermilk out of the icebox and went to the stove to cut a piece of cornbread. The thought of buttermilk and cornbread made my stomach churn. Mama could eat the strangest concoctions. Sometimes she eats Argo starch. I haven't been feeling too good lately, especially in the morning. Mama told me there is some sassafras tea in the pot for me. She said I looked like I needed a tonic. I fixed a cup of tea and sat down.

"Now, Pru, let's talk about what you really want to talk about."

"What's that, Mama?"

"Married life isn't what you thought it would be, is it?"

"No, Mama. I'm not sure Morgan is ready to settle down. He still enjoys going out with his friends and going to parties. I didn't want to talk to you about it because I know you will say I told you so."

"No, I won't say that; but you must realize he is young, even younger than you, and whatever happens, you made a marriage vow and you must keep it. I love your Papa with all my heart, and it hasn't always been easy; but I wouldn't trade it for anything. Is there anything else you want to talk to me about?"

"No, Mama. I can't think of anything else."

"When were you planning on telling me and your Papa that you're in a family way?"

"Mama, how did you know? I just didn't think this was a good time to tell you."

"Why wouldn't I know? I've been pregnant twelve times. I certainly should know."

"Yes, I guess you should. Will you tell Papa for me?"

"No need, he already knows."

I shook my head. I never cease to be amazed at the things Mama has a way of knowing.

"Mama, the baby is due the first of March."

"No, the baby will be a boy, born the end of February," Mama said emphatically.

"We'll just have to wait and see, Mama. You can't know everything."

Quiggels

◆

On a cold day, February 25, 1931, labor pains persistently and rudely made me aware it was time to have my husband call for an ambulance and head for the hospital. He just stood there, he was so scared. I had to scream at him to get him to move. He made the call and the ambulance arrived within twenty minutes. I felt relieved to know it would soon be over. Mama predicted it would be February.

The ambulance attendant drove a few blocks, then stopped abruptly at the railroad tracks. What is going on here? I was panic-stricken, thinking I might have my baby in the ambulance. If I did, I knew Morgan would faint. He could never handle seeing anyone in pain, especially me. He sat beside me, holding my hand and shaking. Even though it was a cold day, he was wet with perspiration. The attendants opened the doors and pulled out a stretcher. When they returned, they were carrying a white man who didn't appear to be conscious. They placed the stretcher next to me. I became more concerned for the man than myself.

I was told he was the switchman who sat in the tower, high above the railroad tracks. He often waved to me from the tower. I had never seen him up close. He wasn't wearing the familiar striped cap he always wore. I would wave to him at least once a month when I walked across the track to visit a friend. He was always so friendly. I never expected that we would share the same ambulance.

The attendant told us the switchman probably had a heart attack. I prayed for him between pains. His breathing is shallow. After what seemed an hour, we finally arrived at City Hospital, the only hospital that accepted colored. Twenty minutes later, my son was born. We named him Morgan Adair, Jr. Morgan Sr. was overjoyed that *his* labor pains were over, and the baby was a boy. So was I. I asked Morgan about the switchman. He said, "He died before we reached the hospital." I grieved for the switchman even though I didn't know his name. My grief for a man I had casually waved to and shared an ambulance with was soon overshadowed by the joy my baby gave me.

Little Morgan was a happy child from the very beginning. He was fat, cuddly and such a combination of Morgan and me that it couldn't be determined whom he most resembled. He grew to be a loving child, and didn't go through the terrible two syndrome. As soon as he was able to talk, he started asking when was he going to have a baby sister. I told him he must pray for one.

Three years later, I was expecting another child, convincing Morgan Jr. that prayer works. I decided to have this child at home.

When my labor pains were a half hour apart, I asked Morgan to take Morgan Jr. to Mama's house and to call the doctor. The doctor arrived an hour later. When the doctor started to examine me, we looked at each other for a few moments, trying to figure out where we had seen each other before. Where had I seen this young, white doctor? Was it at the maternity clinic? I wondered. We both started to talk at the same time.

"Are you Prudence with the long braids and ribbons, who used to live on Station Street?"

It had been years since I last saw him.

"Yes," I said between pains that were coming a few minutes apart. "Are you one of the Butterfield twins who lived across the street?"

"Yes, I am," he replied. We both had questions we wanted to ask; and again, we started talking at the same time.

"You first," he said softly.

"I didn't know you were a doctor! Which one of the twins are you? Do you still live on Station Street? How is your brother and your parents? Do you remember my little bad brothers who were much younger than you but threatened to beat you up?" I didn't know what I was saying at this point as the pains were coming every few minutes and I couldn't hear his answers. I wish there had been more time to talk. Seeing him brought back memories of leaving Homer, Georgia and our first home in Indianapolis. My oldest brother, Thurman, was right when he said someday I would think about Homer and not be sad. I no longer have time to think about it. I have a husband and two children that will require all of my time and attention.

Everyone was excited about the baby. I named her Phyllis after the Negro poetess, Phillis Wheatley. I felt my family was complete with a boy and a girl. There were three grandsons before her, but she was the first female grandchild Mama and Papa had. We doted on her because she was small and sickly. She cried a lot. Little Phyllis soon outgrew her illnesses and began to thrive. I often told my family, Morgan Jr. came out of the womb smiling; Phyllis came out with an inquisitive expression. Morgan hasn't stopped smiling; and Phyllis hasn't stopped asking questions. She and her brother were complete opposites. When she began to walk, nothing escaped her scrutiny. Morgan Jr.'s toys were far more fascinating than her own. She felt, "If I see it, it's mine." One day, after one of her antics, he said, "I'm so sorry I asked God for you!" She didn't understand what he said but she knew he wasn't happy with her.

"Since you're so upset with her, how would you like for me to take her to the park and leave her?" I asked, waiting for his emphatic, "No." I was testing him. To my surprise, he said, "OK, that's a good idea!"

I put my coat on and then Phyllis'. I thought I would walk around the block to give my little six-year-old a chance to realize how much he loved his little sister.

"Wait a minute, Mother," he said, putting on his coat.

"Where are you going?"

"I'm just going to stay with her in the park to make sure somebody picks her up." We both laughed "Maybe we should just keep her."

"I agree," I said. He knew neither of us would ever leave her.

Morgan Jr. was quite content to play quietly with his trucks. Phyllis loved to read. When she was three, she tried to read her books. She would point and ask, "What's that?" attempting to pronounce the name of the person or thing. One day she realized the people in the book didn't look like any people she had seen, but she knew the names of all the characters in her books. There is a white man pictured in the book as a farmer. Phyllis had never seen a white farmer, or any other farmer. She seemed puzzled by it.

Shortly after trying to explain about the white farmer, I called Metropolitan Life Insurance Company to talk about a policy. The company sent out an agent to discuss the policy. He would also collect for it each week. When the agent came to the door, Phyllis ran to the door shouting, "Farmer, farmer!" I suppose she thought, if he's a white man, he must be a farmer. "No," I said; "This is the insurance man; his name is Mr. Quiggels."

Phyllis broke out in gales of laughter; she was holding her little stomach and rolling on the floor. "Quiggels?" she said, "Quiggels?" She couldn't stop laughing. I was so embarrassed, but Mr. Quiggels began to laugh too. He was completely enchanted by this three-year-old cut-up. They became friends and he called her Sweet Pea.

Every Monday, when Mr. Quiggels came to collect for the insurance, Phyllis was waiting with her book. They would sit on the steps in the summer and he would read to her, until years later, when she read to him. He was loving and patient. They had a friendship I sometimes envied. To her, there was no one like Quiggels. As soon as he stepped to the door and said, "Where's my Sweet Pea," she would run and grab his hand and say, "Hi, Quiggels; let's read a story!" This continued for many years.

Every year from the time Morgan Jr. was three years old, I took him to Riverside Amusement Park on Milk Top Day. When Phyllis was old enough, I took her also. We went once a year until Phyllis was eight. The children couldn't wait until "milk top day" at Riverside Park. Admission was based on the number of tops you saved from Polk milk bottles. We boarded the bus, along with friends and relatives, anticipating a fun-filled day at the park. A few hours after arriving at the park, I noticed Phyllis had that inquisitive look (I dread) on her face. "What's wrong?" I asked.

"Why don't we come to the park every week? It would be fun to come every week," she moaned.

I didn't know how to tell her but I knew I had to tell her the truth. I hesitated for a moment. She was waiting for an answer and her expression seemed to say, I don't think I'm going to like your answer. I cleared my throat. "We can only come once a year," I said with a lump in my throat.

"Why?"

"Because colored people are not allowed to come more often than one day a year."

"Who won't let us come?"

"The people who own the park," I answered, hoping that would end the questions.

She was quiet for a moment, then she asked, "Are we colored people?"

"Yes,"

"Are the people that own the park white people?"

"Yes," I said, hoping that this was the last question. I could see she was still thinking and not satisfied with my answer.

"Why don't they want us to come?"

She was relentless and I wasn't prepared; but I knew I had to answer her. "Honey, there are, unfortunately, some white people who don't like colored people; and since they own the park, they can decide who comes to the park and when." I knew I handled it badly but I was sure that settled it for now. I would discuss it later, when I thought she would understand.

She looked up at me, her eyes were narrowed and her jaw was set. "They don't know me, so how can they not like me? I will never come back to this park again. I'm going to talk to Quiggels about this!"

With that announcement, she stomped off to catch up with her friends. I reproached myself for not handling it better. I'm never quite prepared for some of Phyllis' questions; but I will never discourage her from asking. She was quiet all the way home and talked very little over the weekend.

Monday, Phyllis was sitting on the steps, waiting for her friend, Quiggels. When he saw her, he said, "Hey, Sweet Pea, are we going to read a story?"

"No," she snapped and got up and went into the house. I guess she changed her mind about talking.

Mr. Quiggels was taken aback; he had never seen her unhappy and sullen before. "What's the matter with Sweet Pea," he asked.

"Just growing up a little," I said, not knowing how to answer him.

Mr. Quiggels recorded my insurance payment and went out and sat at his usual place on the steps. Shortly, Phyllis came out and sat down beside him. From the sofa in the living room, I couldn't hear all she said, but just enough to know she was talking to him about Riverside Park. I heard her very clearly when she said, "Quiggels, are we friends?"

"Of course," he answered enthusiastically.

"Do you like me even though I'm colored?" she asked in a voice that almost broke my heart.

"No, I don't just like you, I love you, because you're my Sweet Pea; and if I owned that park, I would let you come anytime you wanted to."

I smiled approvingly. She laid her head against his shoulder and they sat silently for awhile. Finally Phyllis got up and came into the house. She didn't tell Mr. Quiggels good-bye. As she passed, I could see her feathery eyelashes glistening from the tears she had not allowed to fall.

When Mr. Quiggels got up from the steps, his face was red and his voice was hoarse as he said, "I'll see you next week, Mrs. Adair." He shouted a good-bye to Phyllis. She didn't answer.

Before he got to the end of the walk and through the gate, Phyllis ran past me, almost stepping on my feet, on past the porch and stopped half way between the porch and the gate. She yelled, "Quiggels, will you *always* be my friend?"

"*Always* and forever, Sweet Pea. *Always* and forever, I promise," he assured her.

She ran and jumped in his arms and said, "Then, I will *always* be *your* friend."

In the years that followed, Quiggels kept his promise, and so did she.

Memories and Mysteries

◆

The house is quiet; I welcome this rare time to relax and think. I wish I could stop time and start it again at the point it was most beautiful for me. Time goes by so quickly; but one of the best things about it is that it really does eventually heal or at least lessen some pain. Trying to forget the unpleasant things is the hardest to do.

Even after all these years, I remember, as if it were yesterday, when Papa received a telegram saying his brother Frank was in the hospital. Papa took a bus to the hospital. When he arrived at the door of Uncle Frank's room, Uncle Frank waved to him and was dead before Papa got to his bed.

After Uncle Frank's funeral, I had never seen Papa so distraught. I thought he was upset when Mama went to Homer but not as bad as this. Papa could not be comforted; he still can't whenever he thinks about it. The worst part for Papa was that Uncle Frank had a pauper's funeral and was buried in a pauper cemetery in an unmarked grave. There was no money. Papa and Uncle Frank had a special bond. They loved each other unconditionally and made so many sacrifices for each other. I don't know who broke the news to Uncle Wes, but whoever it was, I feel sorry for them.

That same year, I received word that Mitchell Brant, the young man I had considered marrying before Morgan, was sick. He has been quite successful on the farm he inherited from his father. Mama was so impressed with Mitchell. Rumor had it that even at his young age, he was one of the richest colored men in Glasgow, Kentucky. Mitchell didn't give up trying to get me to marry him, even after I married Morgan. He told Mama he felt I had made a mistake by marrying Morgan. When I was pregnant with Phyllis, he came to see me at my mother-in-law's house. He wished me well and said he was giving up. I told Morgan but he didn't seem a bit bothered by it.

A few months later, our church went to a convention in Glasgow, and Morgan and I went along. I called Mitchell but he wasn't at home. I'm so sorry he wasn't. I often wonder if I made a mistake by not marrying Mitchell. Mitchell never married and had no children. I am still heart broken when I think about him being found dead, lying across a fence on his farm. There had been a rainstorm and he was struck by lightning. He was in his late twenties. I think I will always miss him. "Why Mitchell, Lord?"

Mama said I must believe that there is a master plan for our lives. Was Uncle Frank's and Mitchell's deaths part of a master plan? Sometimes I don't like God's plan. It makes me mad that I have no say in it. Mama says God works in mysterious ways. I can't disagree with that. I hope there will be no more dying and no more mysteries for awhile. I'll try not to think of it. There have been so many changes in my life since then.

We are now in our third home since living with Morgan's parents. The first one was rented and Phyllis was born there. It was halfway between Morgan's parents and mine. I almost worked myself to death cleaning it up. It had previously been rented by bootleggers. The second was also rented. This is where Phyllis met her friend Quiggels, who has been our insurance man for seven years. We saved money for a down payment for our third house, our present one. It is a small frame, five-room house. The backyard is large. I have a garden; I really enjoy working in it. I have tomatoes, green beans, onions, carrots and radishes. The children love to pick the tiny bite-sized tomatoes. They sneak, or think they are sneaking, them from the garden and toss them, unwashed, into their mouths. I also have beautiful flowers: zinnias, lily-of-the-valley, marigolds, iris, rooster combs, lilac, forsythia, snowball and rose bushes. The children call the large tree in the backyard their cigar tree because the hanging pods look like long cigars. They have built a tree house in it.

My children and my garden are such a consolation to me, both keep me busy. Everyone who is able has a garden because of the war. They call them "victory gardens," and we try to conserve. Mothers are afraid their son, husband, or brother will be drafted. Harold is in the Army and Ralph is in the Navy. Mama and Papa worry about their safety.

Nineteen forty-four is a time of patriotism and sentimentality. When we can, we buy war bonds. Almost everything is rationed; stockings, sugar, gasoline and even shoes. Since nylon stockings are so scarce, the popular thing is to wear queens lace stockings that look like fishnet. Mama says those kind of hose are only worn by loose women. Maybe so, but I sure wish I had a pair. Many of my friends wear leg make-up. I don't know why. They don't need it; but it's the style. Most of my friends wear their hair in a pompadour in front and a pageboy in back, Andrew Sisters style, and so do I. We listen to the radio constantly, trying to find out how the war is going. When we're not listening to the news, we listen to the Andrew Sisters singing *Boogie Woogie Bugle Boy*, the Mills Brothers rendition of *Till Then*, and Frank Sinatra singing everything with the big bands. Men smoke Camel, Lucky Strike and Phillip Morris cigarettes when they can get them. They are rationed too. Morgan smokes Camels. We look for a hero, and always root for Joe Louis whether we like boxing or not. Some people go to movies to escape, and others go to dances and do the Jitterbug. I rarely do either. Movies are a luxury I cannot often afford, and I can't do the Jitterbug. I never even learned to do the Charleston. Thurman never lets me forget that. I don't feel I have missed much. I have plenty to do with my time.

I can't understand how Mama and Papa raised eleven children. Two are as much as I can handle. Morgan makes three. I do often feel deprived of Morgan's time and attention. We have been married for twelve years and Morgan still hasn't changed. Why did I think he would? He still enjoys playing cards and partying with his friends. He's always the life of the party. I must say he does love his children and they love him, but he doesn't spend enough time with them. My friends have told me that Morgan is having an affair. I have had my suspicions. I confronted him but, of course, he denied it. I don't talk to Mama about it. I'm sure she has already heard it. I have stopped arguing with Morgan. He said he isn't going to leave, and neither am I. I didn't realize before we married how different we are. I enjoy the children, church, my Sunday school class, walks in the park and my family. The only interest we share is our children. Morgan Jr. enjoys games, his friends, and *Jack Armstrong the All American Boy* on the radio, and he thinks younger sisters are a nuisance. When I have time, I like to listen to *Stella Dallas, My Gal Sal,* and *Fibber McGee and Molly.* Phyllis likes *Captain Midnight* and has sent away for the secret decoder to unlock the Captain Midnight mysteries.

Saturday is cleaning day and I insist the children help. They don't mind too much. In the afternoon, we take a break and listen to *Let's Pretend* on the radio, which is re-enactments of fairy tales. Mr. Quiggels comes by in the afternoon to collect for the insurance. He likes to listen to my Mahalia Jackson records and visit with Phyllis.

Sundays we always go to church. That is, me and the children go; Morgan stays at home. We go to morning service, afternoon service, BTU (Baptist Training Union) and sometimes night service. One Sunday after attending morning and afternoon service, Phyllis stopped at the door of the church and said, "Please, Mother, can't I just sit on the steps? Why do I have to go to church so much?"

"When you were born, I thought your vision would be severely impaired, or you might be blind."

"Why did you think that?"

"Your eyes were like pools of blood. I continued to take you to the hospital but nothing the doctors did helped. Mama said I was just wasting time because the doctors didn't know what they were doing. She mixed boric acid and some of her other exotic herbs and applied it to your eyes. She said I should keep you out of the light for awhile. We applied Mama's mixture to your eyes and I prayed night and day. I promised the Lord if He would give you your sight, I would give you back to Him by taking you to church as often as I can. After several days and nights of prayers and promises, your eyes cleared up."

"Mother, are you saying that's why I have to go to church so much?"

"Yes, don't you think that's a good reason?"

"Well, maybe, but if you just let me sit on the steps this time, I promise I'll sit here and really…try to think of something I can do for the Lord other than going to church."

I realized my child was getting fed up with church. I cut out the afternoon and night services.

Monday is wash day, one of my least favorite days. In the summer, I always hang the clothes on the line outside. They always seem cleaner when I hang them outside. In the winter, I have to string a line in the kitchen and it makes the whole house feel damp. So, washing in the summer is more tolerable. I have a Maytag washer with a wringer on top. After the clothes are washed, they are fed through the wringer to extract as much water as possible. One day I left the washer running while I went outside to hang up clothes. I heard Phyllis screaming and ran in to see her braid winding around the rollers of the wringer. The rollers had gotten all the way up to her scalp. I hit the top of the wringer and released the rollers. I thought her hair would be pulled out at the roots but she ended up with braid in tact and a very bad headache. I had left the newspaper on the wash tub and when she leaned over to read it, her hair was caught in the wringer. If there is something to read, she is going to read it; but she never read a newspaper leaning on a wash tub again.

Phyllis always manages to make life interesting. She loves to go to the neighborhood grocery by going through the back gate, across the alley and through a vacant lot. Next to the vacant lot lives a couple, the Browns, with two children who appear to be about eight and ten. The children can neither hear nor speak. Both children have a dark complexion; their eyes are a deep Mediterranean blue. I have never seen anyone, colored or white, with eyes like theirs. Phyllis is fascinated by this and stops when she sees them in their backyard when she goes to the grocery. I often stand in the back door and watch her talking to them. I asked her what she said to them and if she thought they understand her. She said she was sure they did.

"What did you talk about?"

"Just stuff," she would say.

I never complained when she came home and the loaf of bread was mashed flat in the middle, caused by her tucking it under her arm when she talked to the "blue-eyed children" about "stuff." The family moved away and I never found out why their eyes were blue, where they moved, or what Phyllis talked to them about. There is another unsolved *mystery*. I wonder if Mama has an answer for this. She probably does but I'm not going to ask because I'm really mad at her. She let Phyllis talk her into piercing her ears.

I have watched while Mama pierced the ears of girls in the neighborhood. First she numbs the ear with ice, then threads with heavy thread a needle that has been sterilized by burning the tip. She pushes the needle through the numbed ear and ties a knot in the string. For three days the string must be moved back and forth so the pierced ear will not heal around it. After the third day, she burns the end of a broom straw that has been cut to about a fourth inch; removes the string and replaces it with the broom straw. After a few days, the ears have healed enough for earrings. I think this is just horrible!

I think Phyllis is too young to wear earrings. Mama would never have let me get my ears pierced at ten years old, not that I would have wanted to. I will never have my ears pierced. I'm also upset with Morgan because he gave Phyllis a small gold ring with diamond chips. Neither of them asked me if it was all right. I know the ring will probably be lost or given away in a few weeks. Sometimes Mama and Morgan can get on my nerves. Phyllis can be pretty trying, too. Why can't she be more like Morgan Jr.?

Since the children are in school, this is an ideal time for me to take training to become a practical nurse. I've always wanted to be a registered nurse; but I don't think I will be able to find the time or the money to do it. Life with Morgan is so uncertain. I must be able to provide for my children if the time ever comes when I must rear them alone. A lot of my friends are taking jobs in factories, but I prefer a job that will allow me to spend as much time with the children as I can.

Morgan told me the other day that he thinks he might be drafted into the Service. Where did he get a fool idea like that? I don't think that can happen. His mother told me, after we were married, that he was born with a brain tumor. She said she overheard doctors discussing euthanasia. She said she told them in no uncertain terms that they weren't going to kill her baby. I guess that's why she has always been so over-protective. There has never been anything to indicate to me that he has any physical handicap. Did Mother Black make a mistake? She surely must have because

Morgan's thinking proved to be correct. He received a letter saying he has been drafted into the Army. How can this be? Has the United States Army made a mistake? I doubt it. Perhaps this is another example of God's *mysterious ways?*

This Cannot Be

◆

There was no mistake, Morgan has been drafted. It seems the Armed Forces is drafting almost every available male. Morgan accepted the news with his usual nonchalance. I hope the Army will teach him some discipline. The good-bye parties given by his friends continued for two weeks, up to the time of his departure. Morgan Jr. and Phyllis gave him a party too. I think they see it as a big adventure, and Morgan sees it as another big party. I will miss him; I can't imagine what peace and quiet will feel like.

Morgan's basic training was at Camp Atterbury in southern Indiana, after which he was sent to France and Germany. He writes often but his letters are short. He has managed to make a tremendous number of friends in Service, just as he has at home. I often hear from his Army buddies. One of the men he met and befriended asked me to write to his wife. I did, and we became friends. Her name is Doris Cabel; she lives in Cleveland, Ohio. I invited her to come to Indianapolis and visit me. I was delighted when she agreed to come. Morgan Jr. and Phyllis liked her right away and started calling her Aunt Doris.

Doris was anxious to see downtown Indianapolis the day she arrived but I am too busy preparing Sunday dinner. So, I told her I would be glad to take her on Monday.

"With a few instructions, I can catch the bus, walk around downtown and return before dark. I'll be fine. Would you mind if Phyllis goes with me?"

"If you can stand Phyllis' questions, *please* do."

Phyllis is excited about going downtown. I am grateful Doris is taking her. This will give me a chance to finish up Sunday dinner.

Morgan has sent pillow covers with the name of every place he has been stationed. The living room is covered with pillows and bric-a-brac from foreign places. Everyone has a flag, usually about 12 x 14 inches with gold fringe, the star or stars on it represent the number of family members you have in Service. My flag has three stars, one for Morgan and the others for Harold and Ralph.

I placed my roast in the oven, straightened up a bit, and sat down for a few minutes. Morgan Jr. was out with his friends, so I leaned back, savoring the moment. I heard someone coming up the walk. Oh no, I was so looking forward to a few peaceful minutes. It is Doris and Phyllis. Doris has a strained expression on her face and Phyllis has that look I always dread.

"What happened, Doris? Why are you back so soon? Did you get lost? Didn't you have a good time?" Doris isn't saying anything.

"Phyllis, what's wrong?" She didn't answer either, but went straight to her room and closed the door.

"Doris, did Phyllis act out?"

"No, Prudence, she didn't."

"Well, what on earth is wrong?"

"I didn't know, Prudence, I just didn't know."

"What is it you didn't know?"

"We were having a wonderful time looking in the shop windows. I asked Phyllis if she would like some ice cream. She said she would love some, so all the way to the drugstore we discussed what kind of ice cream we would get. We tried to outdo each other, thinking of all the different kinds of ice cream. She settled on chocolate. I saw a drugstore in the

Claypool Hotel that looked like a great place to get ice cream. We went in and sat down at the counter. We sat there for about five minutes. There was no one else at the counter and the waitress wasn't busy, so I asked her if she could help us.

'I'm sorry, we don't serve colored people,' she told us in a matter of fact tone. There were no signs, Prudence. I didn't know what to do, so I just came back home. I tried to talk to Phyllis and told her I would find a store and get a whole quart of whatever she wanted and we could all have some."

"What did she say?"

"She hasn't said anything since the waitress told us she couldn't serve us. I just didn't know what to say to her."

"I am furious! How can people be so insensitive." Before I realized what I was doing, I threw every pillow with the name of Army bases on it and jerked the flag out of the window. I know Doris is saying something to try to calm me, but I can't hear any of it. I will do anything to protect my children from prejudice. If I only knew how. I am angry about Riverside Amusement Park, the Claypool drugstore, and about Morgan being drafted to fight for a country that blatantly discriminates. I guess they don't care how it affects innocent children. I ranted and raved until Doris looked almost afraid to speak. I stopped when the door to Phyllis' room opened and she came out; her eyes were red. She walked over and took my hand and patted it.

"Someday it will be all right," she said softly. She picked up the pillows, placed them back on our plastic-covered davenport, and placed the flag back in the window. Then, she returned to her room without another word.

"What an old soul she is, Doris. I hope she's right."

"I hope so, too, Prudence. Should I try to talk to her now?"

"I think not. I think she understands. I wonder if she'll talk to Mr. Quiggels about this."

"Mr. who?"

"Never mind, I think she'll sort it out."

Doris stayed for two weeks and I was sorry to see her leave; so were the children. We had shared so much. We talked about my children and our husbands. I talked to Doris about things I didn't dare discuss with anyone else. We both hoped our husbands would return better than they were before they left.

I don't know what Phyllis told her friend Quiggels. She never mentioned it again. A few days later, Mr. Quiggels knocked at the door. I was surprised to see him because this wasn't his regular day to collect for the insurance.

"Hello, Mr. Quiggels. Won't you come in?"

"Hello, Mrs. Adair. No, thank you; I'm in a bit of a hurry. I'm usually collecting on the West side of town. Is Sweet Pea at home?"

"No, she's visiting a friend."

"Would you please give her this and tell her I said 'Hello'?"

"Yes, I sure will; and thank you. See you next week."

I closed the door and opened the bag Mr. Quiggels had given me for Phyllis. In it was a quart of chocolate ice cream. Thank God for that man!

Morgan has been in Service for a year. He's in France now. I can guess what Morgan is probably up to in France. I don't hold out much hope for him being better when he gets home; he should be home on leave soon.

The children are growing up and keeping me busy. Phyllis is eleven and Morgan is fifteen. I don't know at what age children's personalities are formed. My children have certainly formed their own unique personalities. I often wonder what they will be like when they become adults.

Morgan Jr. spends lots of time with his friends; they are inseparable. They all have matching red plaid jackets. There is Martin, Frank,

Dawayne, Byron, Clarence, William, and Ronald. You rarely see one without the others. They spend their time, when they aren't in school, sitting on each others' porch, laughing, joking and talking about girls. They pretend they have a car no one except them can see. They had someone take a picture of them leaning on their imaginary car. They convinced a few of the gullible, younger kids that the car was there; but they just weren't smart enough to see it. Phyllis wasn't taken in. One evening, as the boys sat around, they thought up another scheme, a lot more serious. They talked about joining the Army. All of them were seventeen, except Morgan Jr. None of them had gotten up the nerve to talk to their parents about it yet. I'm sure I'll hear more about this.

Morgan wrote and said he should be coming home on furlough in a few weeks. I will be glad to see him, and I know the children will. A few weeks later, one of Morgan's friends called and asked to speak to him. He said he had run into Morgan the previous evening at one of their favorite bars. I told the man he must be mistaken. Morgan wasn't in town. It was obvious the man realized he had said the wrong thing. He stuttered, stammered, and said he must be mistaken and hung up quickly. I started calling around and found out Morgan had been in town two days. I was livid. When Morgan did arrive in a cab, I gave him time to dazzle the children with the gifts he brought. After he finished gift giving and telling exaggerated stories about his adventures, I sent the children to Mama and Papa's house. Of course, my parents thought I wanted to spend some time alone with Morgan. They were right, I couldn't wait to tell him not only did I know he had been in town, but I knew who he had been with. There was lots of screaming by me, and lots of denial from him. Morgan said if I didn't calm down he was going to call a cab and leave again. I didn't calm down, so he called a cab and left.

I knew where he was going and the woman he was going to see. I remembered I had a kerosene lamp. I poured the kerosene into a jar, placed it in a bag, and took a hand full of the matches I use to light the kitchen stove. I started out for the streetcar line. When I get there, I'm going to burn her house down with Morgan in it. I boarded the streetcar, and after riding a few miles, my anger dissipated. I realized how utterly ridiculous I was acting. My parents would be so ashamed of me. What am I thinking! I'm a mother and a Sunday school teacher. I stayed on the streetcar and rode to the end of the line, all the while asking for God's forgiveness. When I got home, Morgan was there. He said he was sorry; he would never do that again. I don't know if I believe him but I promised God, and myself, I will never get that angry again. We called a truce during his time home, and he stayed at home most of the time. A few weeks later, it was time for good-byes again. His furlough is over. The children handled it well because they believed he would be back soon, and that meant more gifts.

I have been spending as much time as I can with Mama and Papa lately because Papa hasn't been feeling well. Lois and her husband live right across the street; and we both live just a short distance from Mama and Papa. We can easily go to see about them. Mama and Papa had a phone installed after Uncle Frank passed away, because if something tragic happened, they wanted to be contacted right away. They never forgot receiving the telegram saying Uncle Frank was in the hospital. Papa always felt if he had had a phone, he could have gotten to the hospital in time to say good-bye.

I have been working pretty hard and under a lot of stress; I think I'll go to bed early tonight. Mama said I needed to take Lydia Pinkam tonic. I felt I had been in bed for about an hour when the phone rang. I turned over and looked at the clock. I had gone to bed at 9:00 PM. It is 2:00 AM. Who would be calling at this hour? "Hello-o-o," I said as sleepily as I could in hope that it would make the intruder feel guilty about calling the wrong number at this hour.

"Hello, Prudence; is that you?"

"Yes, Mama, it's me? What's the matter?"

"Get down here right away!"

"What is it, Mama? Is Papa sick?"

Mama hung up without answering; so I got up, bumping into everything, slipped a dress on over my gown, found my shoes and looked in on the children. They were sleeping soundly. I locked the door and wondered if I should stop and get Lois to go with me. I decided not to alarm her. It took just a few minutes to walk the block to Knox Place. It is so quiet; no one is stirring on the street at 2:00 AM, except me. It is warm but windy on this September morning. The only sounds are the tinkling of Mama's wind chime as it moves with the breeze, and the swishing sound the leaves of the weeping willow trees make as the wind blows. Mama opened the door before I reached the porch.

"What is it, Mama; is Papa sick?"

"No, Prudence; he's not sick."

"Well, what is it, Mama; what's wrong?"

"Your Papa is gone."

"Gone! Where, Mama?"

She pointed to the bedroom. What did she mean? How could he be gone if he's in bed asleep? I tiptoed into the bedroom because I didn't want to wake him. He looked peaceful. I gently touched his hand and it was cold. I laid my head on his chest and I heard nothing.

No, No; God, no; please let me wake up. This is a bad dream. This cannot be. It simply cannot be. I sat on the side of the bed, stunned, disbelieving and praying that I would soon wake up from this nightmare. Mama came and sat next to me. She looked like she was in shock. She didn't cry; but rocked back and forth repeating in a whisper, "Will is gone, Will is gone, Will is gone..."

The Wind Chime Made No Sound

◆

Mama kept her promise and never left Papa, but he left her. He left us all. How can we face life without him? His smile warmed us; his soft, gentle voice brought peace. Arguments were settled with just a look. His large hands tilled soil, planted, made tools, toys, wind chimes, and gave so much comfort. Nothing remained the same once he touched it. The words Mama and Papa have been like one word. How can I speak the name of one without the other? The pain I feel is beyond tears. How can Mama get along without Papa? They have been together since she was fifteen years old.

I must call Thurman and Bonnie. Perhaps they will know what to do; I don't. It is so quiet, Mama has made no sound, and neither has the wind chime. Everything is as still as Papa. I called Thurman and Bonnie and stayed until they arrived. I stopped by Lois' house and told her about Papa. I went home to be with the children. When they awoke, I told them their granddaddy had passed away. Their reaction and most events leading up to the funeral are a blur.

Morgan Sr. is still in Service and won't be here for the funeral. Ralph and Harold were notified and the Navy and Army will allow them to come home. Harold is in the hospital. He had been shot eight times in combat; but he will be able to come home. It was decided to hold the funeral at St. John Baptist Church where Mama and Papa are members. The wake will be at Knox Place.

Everybody has come home to be with Mama and to say a final good-bye to Papa. There are wall-to-wall children, grandchildren, other relatives, friends, and neighbors. I am going to slip away for awhile. I'm going to the park to sit under Papa's "crying tree." The three-block walk to the park seemed like a mile. I found the tree, pulled over a bench, and thought about the time we had spent under this tree. We had shared so much. Papa always knew what to say to make me feel better. This will always be our special place. I will come here to feel his presence, although I know I will feel and see his presence in every flower, tree and everything beautiful. There, under Papa's tree, I was finally able to do what we had done here together. I sat alone and wept.

Papa's casket was placed in the parlor, which seemed both natural and strange. Natural because Papa spent so much time there in front of the fireplace. Strange because a casket was out of harmony with the happiness that was always felt in the parlor. Papa looked so peaceful; I prayed no one would say he did, or any other of the trite remarks people make at funerals. I wish I could scream.

It seemed like hundreds of people came to pay their respects. Among them were two tall white men who looked like Papa. I don't think it was my imagination. No one knew them except Mama. I asked her if they worked with Papa. She said, 'No, your Papa knew them a long time ago.' I knew it was something Mama had no intention of talking about, so there was no need to ask about it again.

Throughout the days of grief, Mama was serene, dignified, and gracious. I wondered what she and Papa had talked about the night before he died. Did he try to prepare her for this? I believe he did. After the funeral, I noticed the wind chime Papa made for Mama which always hung on the porch was gone. Maybe it held too many memories for Mama and she asked someone to cut it down.

We had a family meeting and decided to take turns staying with Mama. All of the children are married and have their own homes, but we couldn't let Mama stay in the house alone, even though she said she would be fine. In the months that followed, many family members took turns staying at Knox Place.

I spent lots of time under Papa's crying tree. Mama seemed to mellow. She is no longer the disciplinarian she used to be. Mama tried to discipline her children even after they became adults. She is different with her grand-children. She catered to them and they all loved her and always wanted to be with her.

Seven months after Papa passed away, Mama had a birthday and I wanted to do something for her (or was it for me?). I invited some of her friends to my house to surprise her. I went to Murphy's five-and-ten-cents store and bought her a real 'wind chime.' It had glass cylinders with tiny flowers painted on them. There were wooden birds and butterflies, all sus-pended from a wooden disc. I thought it was beautiful and would make Mama happy. When she saw it, she pretended to be surprised and happy, but I knew immediately I had done the wrong thing. I never saw the five-and ten-cent wind chime again. I know it could never compare to Papa's. How could it!

Papa Would Know What To Do

◆

Morgan finally came home from Service. The war ended after six years and all over the country people were jubilant. In downtown Indianapolis, people were kissing each other and jumping in the fountain on Monument Circle to celebrate.

Morgan does stay at home more than he used to. He said he had enough of travel in Service. After his father had been home six months, Morgan Jr. came to me and said all of his friends were going into Service and he was going too. It was 1946. He is 15. He had forged his father's signature on the papers. I was so upset. He is just a baby! How can I let him go? I would never have thought Morgan Jr. would do this. He has never been a problem. Morgan Sr. said there was nothing we could do and perhaps he would learn to be a man. Nonsense, I thought, he's a long ways from being a man.

Morgan Jr. left with his friends, Frank, Byron, Martin, Lee and Dawayne. Ronald's father would not allow him to go and made him stay to graduate from high school. They were sent to Anniston, Alabama for basic training.

A few weeks later, I woke up feeling very strange; one side of my face and down my arm felt numb. My face was twisted too. I thought I had slept on one side too long. I went to the doctor and after examining me he said I had had a mild stroke. Oh, Papa, I wish you were here. You would know what to do!

I survived the stroke with no permanent damage. Thank God! After the stroke, I didn't have the strength to fight to get Morgan Jr. out of the Army. Morgan and I had a lot of arguments about it. He felt the Army could teach Morgan Jr. far more than we could. Perhaps so, Morgan Sr. did make a few changes for the better after he came back from Service. He stays at home more; but that has its problems too. Now he entertains more. His friends are constantly at the house, eating up my food and lounging on the furniture. He does, on rare occasions, help with the household chores, but it certainly isn't his favorite thing to do.

Every day is a celebration with Morgan. When you ask him what he's celebrating, he says, "It's somebody's birthday and that's reason enough to celebrate." Everybody thinks Morgan is such a charming gentleman. They just don't know what a pain he can be.

Since he's been home from Service, Morgan has started having seizures. He has them occasionally at night and becomes incoherent, shakes all over, and drips with perspiration. The doctor doesn't know why this happens. If he must have them, I'm glad it happens at night. I wouldn't want Phyllis to be frightened by it.

Because of the seizures, Morgan doesn't drive. That doesn't bother him one bit because his friends are too happy to come and pick him up. When he rides the bus, it just gives him another opportunity to make more friends. Ladies in the neighborhood are always calling to say what a joy he is to talk to as they wait for the bus, and what a wonderful husband and father he must be. Little do they know what I have to endure with that man. Lord knows. Sometimes he tries my patience.

I agreed to go to a party with him last Saturday night because he said I never do anything he wants to do. Phyllis was delighted that we were going someplace together. We called a cab and went to the party. I felt ill at ease because I didn't know anyone there. They felt it was unheard of that I didn't smoke or drink alcoholic beverages. The host brought me a coke and made a smart remark about drinking a soda at a party. I just took my soda and sat in a corner, as far away from the crowd as I could. Morgan, as always, was the life of the party. Everyone started asking him to make a toast. He was happy to oblige. He stood up, glass held high, and made a toast using the filthiest language I have ever heard. I was appalled. While they were still laughing, I slipped into the bedroom and called a cab. I watched for it, and when it arrived, I got in and went home. When I got home, Phyllis wanted to know why I was back so soon and where was Daddy. I told her what happened; she laughed and was not sympathetic at all about how Morgan had embarrassed me. I sent her to her room. She thinks her Dad can do no wrong. An hour and a half later, Morgan called to ask what happened. He was having so much fun it took him that long to realize I was gone. The man is going to be the death of me; he couldn't understand why I didn't enjoy the party. He didn't get home until 3:00 AM. Will he ever learn *life isn't a party*?

Alabama Lesson

◆

Morgan Jr. is in basic training in Anniston, Alabama. Why, of all the places in the United States, did the Army have to send my son to Alabama? If Morgan Jr. had been exposed to racism, he never talked to me about it. It seemed to come to Phyllis early. How will he cope with it? Will he tell me about it and ask my advice? Every time Morgan Jr. wrote, with his beautiful penmanship, he only talked about the interesting things he saw and the friends he met.

When he wrote to his friend, Ronald, who was heartbroken because he didn't get to go to Service with the gang, it was a different story. Ronald told us that Morgan said boot training was awful. They had to walk six miles with a full pack on their back; and in the evening, they would sleep outside under a pup tent. He would have one side of the tent and a buddy would have the other. Both sides would be placed together, then a trench had to be dug around the tent in case it rained. The water would run off the tent into the trench. He said one night he was so tired he told his buddy, Martin, if he wanted to sleep under a tent, he was going to have to put it up alone because he was too tired. He said he had never been that tired in his life.

He told Ronald he was excited when he finally got a pass to go into town. He decided to take a bus and see what the town was like. He paid his fare and sat down on the nearest seat. The bus driver didn't start the bus. He just sat there looking through his mirror. Morgan Jr. said he didn't know what was going on. An old man hollered from the back of the bus and said, "Come on back here, son." As soon as he went back to see what the old man wanted, the driver started the bus. The old man asked, 'Where you from, Son?' Morgan Jr. told him. The old man told him about all the things colored people couldn't do in the South. I don't think I could have told him as clearly as the old man who endured it every day.

Morgan Jr. also told Ronald, when they left Alabama, the train went right through the middle of a field of white stuff. Nobody knew what it was. When the train stopped, everyone got out. They were told it was cotton. He had never seen a cotton field. The boys from New York seemed more surprised than anyone and wanted to take a cotton boll for a souvenir. I never told my son how much cotton I picked as a little girl in Homer, Georgia. I must tell him when he comes home. Morgan Jr. told Ronald that leaving Alabama was one of the happiest days of his life. Unfortunately, their friend, Lee, became ill and had to remain in Alabama until he recovered.

I am grateful to Ronald for sharing what my son wouldn't tell me because he didn't want me to worry. I miss him and his friends so much. I think Phyllis does too, but she won't admit it.

Angel Unaware

◆

By the time the Army found out Morgan Jr. was under age, it was time for him to come home. It is wonderful to have him back home again.

Morgan Jr. tried to enroll in high school. He was refused admission because veterans could not attend high school. How strange that sounds; my son a veteran at 17 years old. He applied for several jobs and finally found one in construction, working on Veterans Hospital. After a few weeks, he decided construction work was not for him. His friends had problems finding suitable work too. They met and considered joining the Marines, but decided to join the Navy.

I am depressed; I feel I am a failure as a mother. I started worrying all over again. Morgan Jr. and his friends were happy they wouldn't have to endure basic training a second time. The Navy gave credit for the Army basic training and also promised to help Morgan Jr. finish high school and possibly college if he stayed in Service long enough. Morgan Jr. and his friends were sent to the naval base at Norfolk, Virginia.

Six weeks after he and his friends left for Norfolk, Virginia, I received a letter saying he would be coming home on leave soon. I wrote back to ask how much money he needed to come home by bus. I didn't hear from him. He surprised us and came home on his own. I am delighted to see him. He is far more handsome in Navy blues than he was in his Army uniform.

"How did you get home? Why didn't you write?"

"I didn't want to ask you for the money, so I hitchhiked."

"All the way from Virginia?"

"Not all the way."

I have always thought Morgan Sr. would be the death of me. "Well, how did you get home without money?"

"A nice white man and his family (a wife and son about 8 years old) picked me up in Virginia and let me ride with them all the way to Cincinnati. They shared snacks with me. When we got to Cincinnati, he asked if I was hungry and if I had bus fare to get home from there."

"Why didn't you call me from Cincinnati?"

"There was no need to, and I wanted to surprise you. The man drove me to the bus station gave me $10 and told me to get something to eat and take the next bus home. I thanked him and told him my parents would mail the money to him if he would give me his name and address. He wouldn't hear of it. He wouldn't even tell me his name. He said he just wanted to help because I looked like a fine young man. He said he hoped someone might do the same for his son someday. He was one of the kindest men I have ever met. His wife was quiet, and smiled a lot. She seemed to have no problem with her husband picking me up. Their son was well behaved, and said he might join the Navy someday. I felt a strange relationship to this family. When the family dropped me off at the bus station, I was sorry to leave their company. I thanked them again. The man helped me get my duffel bag from the trunk. We shook hands and I started toward the bus station. When I turned to wave good-bye, they were gone. I still can't figure out how they got away so quickly. As much as we talked during the trip, I don't remember from where they were coming or where they were going. Maybe I was excited about coming home."

"I can't believe you didn't get his name or address."

"I'm sorry I didn't. He just wouldn't tell me."

Morgan Jr. was out the door to see his friends before I could question him further.

I have thought about the man and his family many times. Mama often quoted a verse in the Bible about being aware of how you treat strangers because you may be entertaining angels unaware. Mama could find a Bible verse to fit almost any occasion.

I read a story once about angels appearing in human form to help when they are needed. Were these the angels I prayed would always protect my family? I hope so. Maybe that's a foolish thought. I don't know, but I thank God my son is home safe, even though it is for a short time. He seems so mature. He's not my little boy anymore.

Morgan Jr. is enjoying his time at home. His friends came over and sat on the porch. It was like old times. They spent their time together talking about girls, the places Morgan Jr. had seen, chasing Phyllis away and listening to records. Their favorite singer is Billie Holiday. She is a beautiful colored woman who always wears a gardenia in her hair. I don't understand why she always sounds so sad. I heard she sounds that way because she's on drugs.

I especially don't like her song called *Strange Fruit*. I forbade Phyllis to listen to it. I might as well have been talking to the wall. I walked into the living room after everyone was supposed to be in bed to find her with her ear pressed against the record player. She had turned the volume down low, hoping no one else would hear it. The song that has caused such interest is about a lynching. The "strange fruit" is a black man hanging from a tree. I have heard far too much about that. I don't want my children to hear it. I didn't discuss it with her…just sent her back to bed. I hope she won't understand it. That child is going to drive me crazy. I went back to bed and talked to Morgan Sr. about it. As usual, he thought I was over-protective.

The next day, I emptied Morgan Jr.'s duffel bag. I wanted to wash his clothes before he went back to the naval base. Nothing is as smelly as a boy's dirty socks. I was shocked when I found his clean socks. He had tied them together using condoms like rubber bands. His father needs to talk to him about this! I talked to Morgan Sr. about it. He thought it was funny.

"Prudence, in Service, you learn to make do; and many films are shown explaining the use of condoms."

I didn't bother to reply. I guess fathers don't worry like mothers do. My son is growing up too fast.

Two weeks passed so quickly. It's time for Morgan Jr. to go back to Virginia, and time to say good-bye again. Will I see my son again? Now I know why Mama prayed so much.

"Lord, when I don't know what to do I pray. I repent of being too busy to pray. Thank you for loving me and my family so much. Thank you for the good times and the bad. I know the bad times strengthen my faith. My faith is truly being strengthened these days. Thank you for my husband and children.

It still hurts that Papa is gone. I know Mama is hurting too. I still miss Papa; and Mama isn't the same. I don't want to complain, but there's so much pain lately. I am so worried. I know worry is a lack of faith. Lord, please bring healing. Please protect my son and bring him home safely. Bless and keep my daughter.

There are times when I don't feel I know how to be a mother or a wife. My son has chosen to leave home a second time; and Phyllis asks questions I sometimes can't answer. Morgan Sr. is another problem. Lord, give me patience and a loving spirit.

Forgive me for all the times I've disappointed you. I know how disappointment feels. Thank you for a praying mother and grandmother, who always covered me with prayer. Thank you for your grace and mercy. Bless and keep the family who picked up Morgan Jr. and gave him money to come home. I know you sent them.

In your word it says to delight myself in you and you will give me the desires of my heart. I do delight myself in you, Lord! My desire is to be a good wife and mother. I pray my husband will be the man I know he can be.

Lord, I hear Phyllis calling me. She probably has a question I can't answer. Lord, give me strength!"

"What do you want, Phyllis?" I tried not to sound annoyed.
"Do you think Jr. will send me the Navy pea coat he promised?"
"If you worried him as much as you worry me, I'm sure he will."
"I did…even more," she said with an impish grin.
"Lord, help me. My family is wearing me out!"

Unsettling Times

Phyllis wrote to Morgan Jr. and worried him about the Navy pea coat until he could stand no more. I don't know how he arranged it, but the long awaited coat arrived. Phyllis is the envy of her friends. She thinks she is hot stuff in that coat. She practically sleeps in it. I'll be glad when spring comes so she can take it off.

Morgan Jr. writes interesting letters from Korea and Japan, telling about all he has seen. I'm never sure if he is really telling me the truth about how things are going with him in Service. His friend, Ronald, finished high school and joined the Air Force. I can no longer count on him to tell me what Morgan Jr. is really up to. Morgan Jr. doesn't have a childhood friend who hasn't been in Service, or is on his way. I continuously pray they all come home safely.

❈   ❈   ❈

Spring has finally arrived. It's always good to see the tulips, daffodils and forsythia in bloom. It's getting warmer. Maybe Phyllis will take off that blasted coat. I doubt it!

It has been almost three years since Papa passed away. I don't think any of us will ever stop missing him, especially Mama. She is quieter now, and tries to stay busy. She joined a neighborhood group, belongs to the Church choir, works on quilts, cans fruits and vegetables, and occasionally writes poetry. Her favorite poet is Paul Lawrence Dunbar.

Morgan Sr. has been reasonably quiet these days too. Thank you, God! He loves to sit on the front porch and greet all the neighbors. There is a young man named Robert Watts who often comes over to sit on the porch and chat with Morgan. He is the son-in-law of my friend, Sadie, who lives on the next street. The neighborhood was shocked when Watts was arrested for murder. He has always been polite and personable, and we are very fond of him. It is hard to believe. I try to keep Phyllis from finding out about it. I know she will be upset because she likes him so much. The Indianapolis Star has been covering the story, so I'll hide the newspapers. I talked to Morgan about it. He was disturbed about the story but didn't feel I should try to hide it from Phyllis.

Phyllis seems to be going through some phase. She's really pouty these days. The school says its puberty. Mama said she's getting womanish. Today she came home stomping around like she was annoyed about something.

"Hello, Phyllis."

"Hello."

"How was school?"

"OK."

"Is something wrong?"

"Yes! Is Rotterdam a bad word?"

"No, Rotterdam is the name of a city, I think. I'm not really sure. Why do you ask?"

"At lunch time, I left my lunch on my desk and went to the restroom. When I got back, my cookies were gone. I know the girl who took them, but she wouldn't admit it."

"What does that have to do with Rotterdam?"

"If that girl took my cookies, I hope they Rotterdam teeth!"

I can't believe this child is telling me this. I am speechless. If I had said this to Mama, she would have killed me.

"I know, I know. Go to my room," she said sarcastically.

Before I could say "Yes, go to your room, close the door and don't come out until I call you for dinner (if I decide to)," she picked up all the newspapers from behind the davenport, that I thought I had hidden, and went to her room and closed the door. I didn't bother to tell her daddy about it.

I decided to call Phyllis for dinner. She said she wasn't hungry. She was busy reading those newspapers. I know she'll read every word about the Watts case and ask a million questions.

I was right, she went on and on about it. She cut out and saved the articles detailing the trial. Watts claimed that on the day of the murder he was nowhere near the scene of the crime, but he couldn't prove it. Of course, Phyllis reads the paper in her room. The child is always on punishment for something. She bursts out of her room yelling, "He didn't do it! He didn't do it!"

"What are you yelling about child? Who didn't do what?"

"Robert didn't do it. I saw him that morning. He couldn't have done it."

"How can you be sure? You must be confused. Why do you think no one but you saw him?"

"I don't know. I just know I saw him. He was smiling and friendly like always, and he said to tell you and dad Hello. Why don't you believe me?"

"I believe you, Honey. I just think you might be mistaken about the day."

"I am not mistaken! I saw him. I saw him." Her voice trails off.

I didn't know what to say to console her. Did she want this man to be innocent so badly she imagined she saw him? Did she see him? I didn't question her further. I hope she'll forget it. This trial has been like a dark cloud over the neighborhood. Everyone has been affected by it.

The trial droned on for months and Watts was found guilty. He was sentenced to die in the electric chair. Watts continued to say he was innocent. Phyllis became withdrawn and did not discuss the trial again, but she continued to read about it. I hope this incident will not leave emotional scars. This is a horrible time for everyone.

It's September 1948 and Mama has been ailing a bit. I've tried to look in on her as often as I can. The phone rings; it's Bonnie. I haven't heard from her for awhile.

"Prudence, come to the house right away."

Bonnie never lets you forget she's the oldest sister. She never requests, she demands. I guess I'll never be an adult to her.

"How are you Bonnie?"

"Never mind, just get down here!" She hung up.

I took off my apron and headed for Knox Place. When I got there, Bruce's wife, Mary, was there. I greeted her and asked about her family and if she knew what Bonnie wanted. She told me Bonnie was upstairs with Mama. Mama had moved her bedroom upstairs after Papa died. I got to the stairway and called "Mama," waiting for her to say *come up, Prudence.*

Bonnie came to the head of the steps and said, "Prudence, Mama is gone!"

I didn't need to be told this time what that meant. I steadied myself on the stair railing and held on. I couldn't move. The next thing I remember was Bonnie trying to pry my fingers from the railing. When she loosened my fingers, the paint from the railing was in my palm and on my fingers.

Again, Bonnie and Thurman made the funeral arrangements. Papa died September 19, 1945. Mama died September 28, 1948. The word *gone* has become a terrible word to me. Mama and Papa will never be *gone* to me.

Seeing Mama's obituary in the paper still gave no proof to me that she is no longer here. The obituary said so little about who she really was; but then you cannot record a life in a paragraph. It read:

Mrs. Sallie Mae Knox

Mrs. Sallie Mae Knox, 60 years old, died Thursday in her home, 2241 Martindale Avenue.

A native of Homer, GA., Mrs. Knox lived in the city 25 years. She was a member of the Greater St. John Baptist Church and its women's chorus and Widows' Club.

Funeral services will be at 2 p.m. Monday in Greater St. John Church. Burial will be in Floral Park Cemetery.

Survivors are six sons: Thurman, Boyd, Harold, Bruce, Ralph and Charles Knox, all of Indianapolis; five daughters: Mrs. Blanche Blowe, Mrs. Lois Myers, Mrs. Bonnie Tinnon, Mrs. Prudence Adair, Indianapolis. and Mrs. Willie Frank Reed, Chicago; a sister, Mrs. Ivory Allen, Commerce, Ga., a brother, Wes Barnett, Milwaukee, Wis., and 15 grandchildren.

I know God gives "beauty for ashes, strength for fear, gladness for mourning and peace for despair" (Isaiah 61:3). I am badly in need of all those blessings now.

After Mama's funeral, all of the family was called to meet at Knox Place to decide what to do with the property. I lived close, so I arrived early. I walked around the yard, looking at the flowers and weeping willow trees that Mama and Papa loved so much. I went inside the house and looked around, and thought of all the Thanksgiving and Christmas dinners I shared with my family. The quiet was unbearable. Knox Place has always been a noisy place. I pulled out the doors that slide into the wall. These doors separated Mama and Papa's room from the living room. As a child, these doors always fascinated me because they were hidden once they were pushed between the walls. My children loved the doors too. I walked into the living room and sat in the over stuffed chair in front of the fireplace. On the mantle are ceramic King and Queen figurines. They are sitting on a throne and their heads bob up and down when you touch them. These figurines have also held an attraction for me. I think Bonnie bought them. I wish I could get up and touch them to watch their heads nod up and down but I'm so tired.

It has started to rain. I'm early, so I'll just wait here for the others. I've never spent time sitting in this big chair. It's so comfortable everybody always fought over sitting in it. It's Papa's chair. I feel close to Papa here. I slide my hand down the side of the chair and Papa's corncob pipe is there. I can still smell the tobacco and see the teeth marks on the pipe stem. Did Papa hide it here, or did Mama put it there to remember him?

The rain is so soothing. What is that sound? It sounds like Papa's wind chime. Did someone put it back up? I'm so tired, I can't get up to see. Where is that light coming from? I see before me a large field. No, it's not a field. It's the churchyard in Homer. There's the Kings Branch Church. There's Mama in the little graveyard next to the church, sitting on the ground. She is wearing a long blue print cotton dress and a matching kerchief around her hair. And, she is holding something. What is it? If only I could see…I can see now! Mama is holding a baby. The baby is very small. It must be a girl because the baby is dressed in pink. What a beautiful baby it is. Brown curls show from under her lace bonnet. Her eyes are a smoky blue, like Papa's. Her tiny fingers open and close as if she is grabbing the air. Is this Mama's first baby, Isa May, who died after nine days? I don't understand. I see someone coming down the road. It's Papa! He has on bib overalls and he's smiling. He walks over to Mama and the baby and lifts her and the baby so easily. They are starting to leave the churchyard now. Someone else is coming. I can't make out who it is yet. It looks like Miss Abigail. She looks the same as she did when I last saw her, when we were leaving Homer. Her long gray hair hangs loosely to her waist. The hem of her long white dress is covered with red dust. I'm so glad they are together and… There's the sound of the wind chime again, and another noise.

"Prudence, Prudence, come to the door! Are you asleep in there?"

I guess I had fallen asleep. I rubbed my eyes and stretched, then got up and went to the door. It is my brother, Ralph.

"Prudence, did you go to sleep? I've been calling you and tapping on the window for five minutes. Why are you looking so strange?"

"I suppose I did fall asleep."

"Did you have a good dream?" Ralph asked with a smile.

"I'm not sure it was a dream, but it was very good."

"Tell me about it."

"I'm not sure you would understand. I'm not sure I do, but I hope this dream comes true."

Temporary Reprieve

◆

The family arrived and we laughed and cried and talked about Mama and Papa and all the good times we have shared. Knox Place is alive again, at least for awhile. I didn't tell them about my dream. I was afraid it might make them sad. Besides, I just don't want to share it; maybe I'll tell them about it someday.

We decided to keep the house and planned to convert the upstairs into a small apartment. The income would help to maintain the property. Ralph will move in. Everyone felt comfortable with this decision. None of us could bear to part with the house.

Morgan Jr. is still in Service and Phyllis is a typical teenager. She loves loafer shoes with a shiny penny inserted in an opening on top, dirty saddle oxfords with names written on them, and bobby socks. She must have bangs that cover her eyebrows and her hair in a ponytail. The styles teenagers wear are just terrible. The slang is even worse. Of course, Phyllis uses slang. I read in the paper the other day about a lady who spoke several languages. She said it is a natural thing for young people to develop their own way of talking, but she didn't understand any of it either. When I was growing up, I don't remember having a different language. Well, I guess she will outgrow it.

Phyllis still reads the paper about the Watts trial, but I can't get her to talk about it. I know she is still bothered by it. The paper said the murder and attempted rape took place at the home of Mr. & Mrs. Burney on November 12, 1947. Mrs. Burney was found by her husband and a neighbor at 6:00 in the evening, clad in a nightgown and robe. A butcher knife was found near the body; and a 16-gauge shotgun, that belonged to Mr. Burney, was missing. The police said Watts admitted killing Mrs. Burney, and led them to the place where he threw the shotgun. He was in custody when Mrs. Burney's body was found.

The police also said they found Watts' jacket at the home of Mrs. Stout, who lived a few blocks from the Burneys. She said Watts knocked on her door and asked to use the phone. When she let him in, he tried to attack her. She was able to get away and ran out the door and called the police. Watts was arrested, questioned, beaten and charged as a vagrant although he had a home and was picked up on his job at the City garage where he drove a truck for the City. The police said Watts left the Stout residence and went to the Burneys, gaining entrance the same way he had at Mrs. Stout's. He struggled with Mrs. Burney; she grabbed a shotgun, it went off, blowing away her face.

The police questioned Watts about every murder case that hadn't been solved. Two weeks before the Burney murder, another woman was murdered. She was stabbed in the throat with a butcher knife. Her name was Merrifield. Watts could not be connected to this murder.

The police described Watts as being cocky. He never seemed that way to me. Morgan doesn't believe Watts murdered Mrs. Burney. He said Watts knew her well and wouldn't have killed her. I sure hope he didn't do it. I feel sorry for his family. He has 14 sisters and brothers. Watts is only 27 years old. I suspect his mother and wife must be devastated.

Two months later, January 1948, the trial was held in Shelbyville, Indiana. The jury was out for only four hours; and Watts was sentenced to die in the electric chair for the Burney murder. February 2, 1949, Watts' head was shaved to prepare him for execution. The N.A.A.C.P. (National Association for the Advancement of Colored People) intervened before the execution and Watts was granted another trial which would take place in a few months. Thank God!

The trial wasn't discussed for awhile, at least not in Phyllis' presence. Morgan and I discussed it often after we went to bed. I was almost pleased when Phyllis' interest turned to make-up, movies and boys.

Morgan stays at home more than he used to; maybe he's maturing. Occasionally he stays out late. When he does, he always takes his shoes off at the door, tips in and undresses in the dark. He sits on the side of the bed and waits for me to fuss at him for not calling to tell me he will be late. I usually don't say anything. I pretend I'm asleep. He always says: "I know you're not asleep, Pru. If you were, you would be snoring." I don't answer; I'm just glad he's home. Sometimes he won't stop talking until I talk to him. I think he feels guilty and wants me to fuss at him. Morgan feeling guilty about anything is certainly a change.

Tonight Morgan is late and he didn't call. I hear him as he opens the door, and I look at the "Glow-in-the-Dark" clock. It's after midnight. Morgan comes in and sits on his side of the bed.

"I know you're awake, Pru. I want to talk to you."

I am not going to answer him. He pulls back the cover and starts tickling my feet. He knows I can't stand that. He tickles me until I have to talk to him. "Stop it," I laugh. "Do you know what time it is?"

"Yes. I've got something to tell you and you are not going to believe it!"

"You're right, I probably won't. What is it?"

"You know, at the shop we take care of most of the cleaning for business people downtown"

"Yes, I know that."

"Well, did you know when there is a stage show at the Circle Theater, we also clean the costumes."

"No, I didn't know that. But what's that got to do with you getting home so late?"

"I'm getting to it. The cleaning for the actors wasn't picked up. Since I pass the theater on my way home, I volunteered to drop it off. I went to the stage door and told the doorman I had cleaning from the Star Service Shop. I thought the doorman would take the cleaning, but he asked me if I would take it to Mr. Lorre's dressing room. I knocked on the door, and Peter Lorre opened the door and asked me to come in."

"Who is Peter Lorre?"

"Pru, don't you know anything? Peter Lorre is a movie star. You need to get out of the house more. I bet Phyllis knows who he is."

"She probably does, she spends every Saturday afternoon at the movies. What does he look like?"

"Well, he's short, has a short neck and a wide forehead, and has large sleepy eyes. He is soft spoken and has a nice smile. He smokes and drinks a lot—more than I do."

"Morgan, that's not possible!"

"That's what you think."

"You have come up with some stories, but this is the best yet. You still haven't explained why you're late."

"I'm trying to; hold your horses. Mr. Lorre invited me to sit down and have a nightcap with him. I did and we had a wonderful time. I really enjoyed talking to him. He sent out for sandwiches, and before we realized it, it was almost midnight. There were no more busses, so he called a cab for me and paid for it."

"This is your best story yet, Morgan. Now, can I go to sleep?" He was still talking when I dozed off.

The next day, I asked Phyllis if she had ever heard of Peter Lorre.

"Sure," she said. "Why?"

I don't know why you can't ask that child a question without her asking you one. I told her what Morgan had told me. My, was she excited.

"Tell Dad to get an autograph!"

"I don't think it's likely he will see him again."

"Aw rats!" she said disgustedly.

"I don't like that expression, Miss."

She picked up the newspapers and went to her room. She's probably still keeping up with the Watts trial. The latest development is the new second trial. The N.A.A.C.P. got involved because his civil rights had been violated. He had been beaten into confessing to the Burney murder and the Merrifield murder.

Phyllis interrupted my thoughts by yelling, "Don't forget to tell Dad to try to get an autograph from Peter Lorre."

I guess she paid no attention when I told her it wasn't likely Morgan would see him again. She has a way of hearing only what she wants to hear.

Morgan is late for dinner again! Phyllis is disappointed because she didn't get a chance to talk to him about Peter Lorre. It's midnight and I hear a car drive up. I get up to see a cab leaving, then jump back in bed. I don't want Morgan to know I never go to sleep until he comes home.

Morgan comes into the bedroom, quietly changes to his pajamas and sits on the bed. "OK, Pru, stop playing 'possum. I know you're not asleep."

"No, I'm not asleep. Phyllis was disappointed when you didn't get home for dinner."

"She'll forgive me when she finds out what I brought her."

"What did you bring her?"

"I told you I brought it for her. You'll see it when I give it to her in the morning."

"What's your reason this time for not getting home in time for dinner?"

"Mr. Lorre called the shop and asked if I could drop his cleaning off again. I didn't mind. He's very easy to talk to."

"I still can't imagine what you could possibly have to talk to him about?" I don't know why I asked. Morgan could get conversation from a rock.

"This time he talked about his career and seemed really interested in the places I had gone to in Service. He asked me if I would consider traveling with him and being his dresser. He said he would triple whatever I made."

"What did you say?"

"I said I would think about it." When Morgan saw my expression, he said, "I'm just kidding. I told him I had enough of traveling when I was in Service and I wanted to be at home with my family."

"What did he say about that?"

"He said he understood; but if I changed my mind, just contact him. So you better watch your 'Ps & Qs,' Pru. I might decide to take him up on it some day."

"Don't let the door hit your backside when you leave," I said.

"You know you would miss me," he said teasingly.

I would, but I 'm not going to admit it to him.

The next morning, Morgan woke Phyllis. I heard her yelling and jumping up and down.

"What on earth is your problem, child?"

"Look at this! It's a twenty-dollar bill. Look what's written on it!" she said excitedly.

"If you will stop jumping up and down, I will."

"To My Darling Niece, Uncle Peter." Under that message, Mr. Lorre signed his name in full: Peter Lorre. She didn't eat breakfast because she couldn't wait to get to school to show off her prize. Morgan became a bigger hero to her, if that's possible. When she got home from school, I asked her if everyone had seen the twenty-dollar bill.

"Not everyone. I still have a few more people to show it to. I thought I was in trouble in my English class."

"Why? What happened?"

"I was passing the twenty-dollar bill around so some of my classmates could see it. The teacher caught me and told me to bring what I was passing around so she could see it. I knew I was in trouble, but she said: 'Is this **The** *Peter Lorre*?' When I said, yes it is, she started telling us about Peter Lorre's pictures and how much she liked a movie called "Black Angel," with Dan Duryea and Broderick Crawford. Then she kept repeating: 'That's power. That's power.' I don't know what she meant by that but I was happy not to be in trouble. Talking about Peter Lorre was a lot more interesting than diagramming sentences."

Before I could scold her, she was out the door, calling back: "I'll be back for dinner. I'm just going across the street to show the twenty-dollar bill to my cousins."

Thank God for a few minutes of rest. It's always something with that girl. Last week a teacher sent her to the nurse with a note saying her nails were too long. Needless to say, she was upset when the nurse cut them. I can't say I blame Phyllis; but if I agree, she will never stop talking about it.

Morgan just got home. I'm surprised to see him home on time. That ended my few minutes of rest. He said hello and asked if Phyllis had calmed down yet. I told him she hadn't. He went into the living room, turned on the radio and waited for dinner.

The phone rang. "Will you get that, Morgan?"

"Why don't you get it? I'm listening to the news."

"Whatever you are listening to can't be more important than dinner, can it?"

He wasn't moving, so I answered the phone with flour on my hands. I knew it would be for Morgan. I don't know how his friends always know when he's at home. "Hello."

The caller said, "Hello, Mrs. Adair, how are you?"

"Fine," I answered.

"May I speak to Morgan?"

"Just a moment!" The voice was unfamiliar to me, kind of soft and strange. "Morgan, telephone!"

"Who is it?" he asked, trying to whisper.

"I don't know."

"Well, ask!"

"Hello, may I ask who is calling?" I resent going through this when I have dinner to fix.

"This is Peter Lorre. Please tell him I'll only keep him a moment."

I dropped the phone, picked it up, apologized and told him Morgan would be here right away. I placed the phone down softly and told Morgan to "*hurry up*, it's Peter Lorre!"

Morgan took his time getting to the phone.

"Hello. Just fine, and you? Yes, I enjoyed talking to you too. She's fine. She has shown that twenty-dollar bill to everyone. I'll tell her. No, I haven't changed my mind. I will. I appreciate that. No, I won't forget. Good luck to you too. Take care of yourself. Good-bye."

I stood there with my mouth open for a moment. Morgan didn't seem a bit excited about it, as if he talked to a movie star every day. When Phyllis got home and found out she missed a chance to talk to Peter Lorre, she couldn't eat dinner.

After a few weeks, when everyone she knew had seen and handled the famous twenty-dollar bill, spending it became far more important. The badly worn bill was spent for make-up, a sweater, skirt, shoes and, of course, movies. Maybe life will get back to normal around here— whatever normal is. The Peter Lorre excitement did take our minds off the Watts trial for awhile. Peter Lorre will never know the joy he brought to my child. It was a temporary reprieve from the grief and confusion I know she feels.

The second trial for Watts was held March 1950 in Columbus, Indiana. This time, six women came to the trial and identified him as the man who had attacked them. I don't know why they weren't present at the first trial. The paper said Watts became uncontrollable and had to be restrained. I think it was because he probably had never seen any of them before. He protested many times during the trial.

After the second trial, the N.A.A.C.P. washed their hands of it and said Watts had received a fair trial. He was sentenced to death in the electric chair a second time. Monday, January 15, 1951, Watts' head was shaved again and his pant legs slit to prepare for electrocution. The newspaper said he couldn't believe the N.A.A.C.P. wasn't going to help him again. A group of ministers appealed to Governor Shricker for clemency, claiming Watts was mentally ill. The Governor turned it down. Watts continued to say he was innocent.

Finally, Watts was resolved and lost hope. His wife divorced him while he was on death row. Prior to the execution, he tried to puncture an artery in his arm with a pencil. The puncture was discovered and the wound was bandaged.

January 16, 1951, the headline read; *Watts Goes To Chair*. The paper said the trial had cost the state $200,000 and $25 for the electrocution. Watts went to his death still denying any guilt. According to the paper, he walked calmly to the chair. His last words were: "Lord have mercy on me according to thy loving kindness." He was given 2,200 volts of electricity, which evidently didn't kill him. Then, he was given 440 more volts; then an additional 220 volts. Three minutes later, he was dead. He died three years and three months after the death of Mrs. Burney.

I wish the paper hadn't printed the details of the execution. Watts willed his only possession, his Bible, to his mother who lives in Chicago. The body was sent there for burial.

When Watts went to prison, there was another man named Lobough on death row who had admitted raping and killing two women. He was given numerous stays of execution. This admitted killer was still on death row when Watts went to the chair. I wonder why there was such a hurry to put Watts to death. Perhaps, if there had been more time, he might have been proven innocent. There are some things the Lord will have to help me understand.

The neighborhood is stunned. My child is broken hearted and will never believe Watts was guilty. She still won't talk about it, but silently grieves. I pray that in time it won't hurt her anymore.

Like Mama, when I am in need of strength, I can always find it in the book of Psalms:

The righteous cry, and the Lord heareth, and he delivereth them out of all their troubles. The Lord is nigh unto them that are of a broken heart; and saveth such as be of a contrite spirit. Many are the afflictions of the righteous; but the Lord delivereth him out of them all. **(Psalm 34:17-19)**

Trying To Move On

◆

We have tried hard to put Watts' execution behind us. What else can we do? As Mama always said, "There are some things only God can take care of." I believe that's true.

A few months after the Watts incident, like millions of other families, we bought a television set! It is so exciting to Morgan and Phyllis. They watch for hours. I can't get worked up about it. I have too much to do to sit in front of that round tube watching Kukla, Fran & Ollie. I'm not sure television will catch on because you have to sit down to look at it. With radio, you can walk around and get work done while you're listening. I think television gives people an excuse to sit down and mindlessly watch. I don't think it can ever replace the good programs on the radio. I do wish Mama and Papa had lived to see it though.

Morgan and his friends are excited over a colored prizefighter named Sugar Ray Robinson. He is the middleweight champion. What is it about men that makes them always talk about sports? If the man is colored, they really go crazy. Maybe they are looking for a hero. Now, they clutter up my living room watching sports. They used to sit on the porch.

In 1952, the Korean War ended. Thank the Lord! So many boys, colored and white, died in that war. I don't even know what the war was about. Morgan Jr. went to Korea, but he and his friends came home without seeing any combat. A few days after returning home, he received some bad news. Everyone in the company he had been in was killed in combat. All of his friends he went into Service with got home safely. I prayed for the families of those boys.

Morgan Jr. is now discharged from the Navy and he married his child-hood sweetheart. I find it so hard to think of him as a man. He was at home for only fifteen years. That wasn't enough time, but he seems none the worse for it. Maybe the experiences in Service were good for him.

1954

This year, I read in the paper that the Supreme Court made a decision to prohibit segregation in public schools. Making the decision is one thing, but abiding by it is quite another. Phyllis went to an all colored grade and high school. I have often wondered why the fact that her school was not integrated never occurred to her. If it had, I'm sure she would have questioned it. She was probably too excited about going to the basketball games. Attucks High School had one of the best basketball teams in the state, I heard. Basketball doesn't excite me.

I was thrilled when Marian Anderson became the first colored person to perform at the Metropolitan Opera House. I don't understand opera, but Marian Anderson sure does sing Negro spirituals beautifully. Now that's something to be proud of.

1958

It's been seven years since Watts died. I thought time would bring healing for Phyllis, but I don't think it has.

It seems like only a few months ago when Phyllis was getting married. And now, she is unhappy, and I don't know how long the marriage will last. Young people don't stay in marriages, regardless of how bad they are, like my generation. I'm not sure they should. Life is too short to be miserable. She told me she was looking for relief from her problems and went to a movie called "I Want To Live," starring Susan Hayworth. That was a big mistake. She came by and told me about it. Susan Hayworth played the part of a party girl. There was a murder and she was arrested for the murder. She was innocent but the jury found her guilty and she was sentenced to die in the gas chamber. The old Watts memories came back, and she was depressed again. This was certainly not a picture for her to see when she was already down about the possibility of divorce. I like movies about as much as I like television—and that's not much.

A few months later, Phyllis said she is definitely getting a divorce and is considering asking for her maiden name to be restored. "Irreconcilable differences," she said. Why not say you just don't get along? She didn't ask my advice and probably wouldn't have taken it. So…I just listened and tried to be supportive. She said she had already talked to a lawyer and would go to court in a few months. She would need two character witnesses. The witnesses cannot be relatives, and must be someone who has known her for years.

"Who will you ask to be a character witness?" I asked.

"I think I'll ask your friend around the corner, Mrs. Bledsoe, and, of course, Quiggels."

"I know Mrs. Bledsoe will agree, but do you think Mr. Quiggels will take time from his job to go to court for you? He doesn't collect insurance payments anymore. He works out of the office."

"Sure, he'll do it," she said. There was no doubt in her mind that her old friend would be there. She was right.

The day arrived for Phyllis' divorce. I talked to her on the phone just before she went into the courtroom. She sounded really nervous. After the hearing, Phyllis stopped by. She was visibly shaken. I was almost afraid to, but asked cautiously, "How did it go?" She sat down and collected herself, not answering for a while. Then, she started smiling.

"Everything went very well. The judge listened to my attorney with little reaction. He asked for character witnesses, and Mrs. Bledsoe was first. The judge asked her name and if she knew me. She said my parents had been her neighbors for years and she has known me since I was a little girl. The judge listened, then asked in a monotone if there was another witness. I think he thought there wasn't another witness since there wasn't another colored person in the courtroom. I could see him looking around. My attorney said, Yes, Your Honor, there is another witness."

"Quiggels took the stand. He has become even more handsome in the last twenty years. His hair is a glowing white. His eyes are a bright blue, and the wrinkles around them give the blue emphasis. He was impeccably dressed in a navy blue suit, white shirt, striped tie, and highly polished shoes. Quiggels is a man with presence and the judge was impressed."

"While looking over the top of his glasses, the judge asked Quiggels his full name and occupation. Quiggels answered his questions. Then the Judge asked how he knows me. Quiggels looked at me, smiled and said, I met Phyllis when she was three years old, over twenty years ago. She has taught me a great deal over the years."

"Tell me again, Mr. Quiggels, what did you say you do for a living?"

"I work for Metropolitan Insurance Company."

"Could you tell me your relationship to the plaintiff."

"As I said, Your Honor, I have known her for over twenty years. I have loved her since she was three years old. She is my friend."

"Why are you her friend?" the Judge asked.

"Because I promised," Quiggels said. His voice was soft and he was trembling a bit.

The Judge looked at Quiggels with a puzzled expression, then looked at me. He smiled, picked up his gavel, hit it down hard on the podium and said, "Divorce granted!"

"My attorney seemed a bit disappointed that he didn't get a chance to say everything he had prepared; but I was relieved it was over. Quiggels was crying and so was I. I told him good-bye and thanked him for taking time to be in court with me. Mrs. Bledsoe was crying because we were crying. I thanked her too, and called a cab so she wouldn't have to catch the bus. She is such a sweet lady. Good old Quiggels. I don't know what I would do without him."

Phyllis becomes quiet and seems to have forgotten I am in the room. I will leave her to her thoughts. I'm sure it's been a trying day. I thought about Mr. Quiggels—this good and decent man—and wondered what made him the loving man he is. He has been such an important part of my child's life. Without him, I wonder if she would have become bitter. I'm glad I didn't have to find out. In spite of all my children have gone through, I think they will be just fine.

Changing Times

I've been reading a lot lately about a young, colored preacher from Georgia leading boycotts against racial segregation. I sure hope he can do something about it. It would be a good feeling to know someone from my home state can make a difference. Things don't get any better for colored people—They seem to get worse. The 1950's are terrible times for race relations; but at least it is being discussed and recognized as a problem. Perhaps this will be the year something positive will be done.

❄   ❄   ❄

We have a new President, John F. Kennedy. Prior to his election, I read in the paper that he is Irish Catholic and 43 years old. You would think from some of the articles that being 43 years old and Irish Catholic is some kind of crime. I'm glad he's a Christian. Maybe he can end some of this racial stuff. I like him and think he'll do a good job. We need a young man to run this country. The vice-president, Lyndon B. Johnson, is from Texas. I don't know what to think of him yet. I don't think a President from Massachusetts and a vice-president from Texas are going to agree; but what do I know about politics.

President Kennedy has increased the United States presence in Vietnam. Now, here is another war I don't understand. Why are our boys in Vietnam? I had never heard of it before the war there, and I don't know where it is. I tried to discuss it with Phyllis the other day and she went into a tirade. She feels the United States has no business in Vietnam, and young men are dying for no purpose. A few of her friends died in the Korean War. I guess that is why she feels so strongly about it. I was sorry I asked her. The girl can never be accused of not having an opinion.

The news is interesting these days. President Kennedy has set a goal for landing on the moon before the decade is over. I'm starting to change my mind about this young man. Not long ago it was more troops in Vietnam. Now, it's going to the moon. We haven't lost anything in Vietnam or on the moon. I just can't understand why we are going to either place.

The Supreme Court ruled prayer in school is a violation of the first amendment. I can't believe it! I'm glad Mama and Papa didn't live to see this. Mama would say we're going to hell in a handbasket. I never have known what that meant, but we are morally going downhill. If some kids don't have prayer in school, they may not have it any place else. I'm glad I kept my children in church, whether they liked it or not.

The University of Mississippi was forced to admit a colored student named James Meredith the other day. We saw a lot of it on television. It is shameful; state troopers had to be on hand to keep order. I couldn't allow my child to go through all the hardship Meredith will probably have to endure. At least he is an adult. Maybe he can handle it. I know somebody has got to do it.

A neighbor told me Phyllis was in a march, demonstrating against racism. Why am I not surprised? The neighbor said a group marched from St. John Baptist Church to downtown Indianapolis, and it was a peaceful march. I asked Phyllis about it. She played it down as if it was nothing. What can I do? She's grown now.

Martin Luther King, Jr. is leading civil rights marches all over the South. There have been sit-ins and boycotts even here in Indianapolis. I have seen on television police turning dogs and hoses on colored people in the South who only want to vote, eat and live like everyone else.

I have changed my mind somewhat about television. If we didn't have it, we would never know about things that are happening in the world. On the other hand, some times I wish I didn't know.

I am excited about the March on Washington, planned by Martin Luther King, Jr. and other ministers, colored and white. I will certainly be watching that on television. When the day came for the march on Washington, I called all my sisters and brothers to see if they were watching. I called Lois first; she was watching. Then, I called my baby brother, Charles. I knew he would be at home because he has been ill. My other brothers and sisters were working. They probably didn't feel they could take a day off to watch the march. I know it will be repeated, but I couldn't wait to see it.

The spectacle was far more than I could ever have imagined. Thousands of people came to hear Martin Luther King, Jr. speak. It was more of a sermon than a speech. I will never forget the part about wanting his children to be judged by the content of their character and not the color of their skin. That is certainly what I have always wanted for my children. I couldn't be prouder of Dr. King if he was my son.

Morgan doesn't seem to be as interested in following what is happening with civil rights. The only time I can remember he was upset about it was when he was in Service and heard about the German prisoners of war being sent to concentration camps in the South, seated in the front of the train. Colored soldiers had to sit in the back. He was really steamed up about that and I sure couldn't blame him. I think he feels you can't do anything about it, so why worry. He thinks I worry too much. He's probably right. Phyllis tells me every time she visits that worrying is a sin. I don't know where she got that. Maybe I did make her go to church too much!!

When Morgan got home, I told him what Phyllis said.

"She's right, Pru; you do worry too much. It probably is a sin. Almost everything is!"

"I knew you would agree with her. You always do."

"No, I don't. What else did she say?"

"I was ironing some clothes for a neighbor who has been sick when she came in. She said, 'It is awful that you are ironing so many clothes for a neighbor. You should get more rest.' I told her maybe I will be an angel when I get to heaven. 'I have never read about any female angels,' she said."

"What did you say to that?"

"I said I'll just have to talk to the Lord about that when I get to heaven."

"I'll probably get there before you do; so I will talk to the Lord for you, and let you know."

"Morgan, what in the world makes you think you will go to heaven?"

"Why not? I'm not such a bad fellow. I think I have about as good a shot at it as some of your sanctimonious church friends."

"Morgan, if I were you, I wouldn't get my hopes up about heaven."

"Don't be so sure, Pru; you never know."

1963

The world is in shock. President Kennedy was shot and killed in Dallas, Texas. He had been such a champion for civil rights. For the first time, I sat for hours in front of the television, hoping it wasn't so, that a mistake had been made. Grown men cried while watching the funeral procession. It was so touching when President Kennedy's young son, John-John, saluted his father as the funeral procession passed. These are dark days. I thought it couldn't get any worse, but it did.

A man named Lee Harvey Oswald was accused of shooting the President. I was watching television when I saw the police escorting Oswald to or from jail (I can't remember which). A man, later identified as Jack Ruby, stepped from the crowd and shot point blank, killing Oswald. I couldn't believe my eyes. I have never seen anyone killed. The whole world was watching. Is this the beginning of the end of the world? This is unbelievable, like a bad movie.

Lyndon B. Johnson was sworn in as the 36th United States President. Time will tell what kind of President he will make. I wonder if this will change some of the progress that has taken place with civil rights.

1964

March of this year, I read Peter Lorre died. He was 64 years old. Morgan was so sorry to hear it. He invited his friends over to toast the memory of his brief friendship with the actor. Anything is a reason to have a toast with Morgan. I told Phyllis about Peter Lorre. Like Morgan, she was sorry. She said she still had the sweater she bought with the twenty-dollar bill he sent her.

"It's time to give that old sweater a rest. Maybe I should bury it," she said.

I read the newspaper a lot these days. There is so much going on. I don't take time to watch television unless it's something really important. I read that the U.S. Surgeon General reports that cigarette smoking is hazardous to your health. I told Morgan. I thought he might think about stopping smoking those Camel cigarettes. I get so tired of emptying ashtrays.

He said, "You have to die of something. Why not cigarettes? Why don't you read something interesting in the paper sometimes?"

"What do you consider interesting?" I asked

"How about Muhammad Ali defeating Sonny Liston for the heavyweight championship?"

"Who is Muhammad Ali?"

"See, Pru; that's exactly what I mean."

The man is impossible, I thought. I didn't even tell him when I read Lobaugh, who was on death row when Watts was electrocuted, is still in prison. He has had numerous stays of execution. It's been 13 years since Watts died. I'm certainly not going to mention it to Phyllis.

❧   ❧   ❧

1965

I see my brothers and sisters often. We still get together, but it's not the same without Mama and Papa. I see Lois almost every day because she still lives across the street. Lois has three children, two boys and a girl. When we get together, we talk about our families and current events. I always hoped Thurman would have lots of children who would torment him the way he did us. He didn't stop even when we became adults. He only had one son who is a very nice young man. Thurman doesn't deserve that the way he harassed us.

I guess Bonnie was so sick of helping raise us she didn't want any children. So...she doesn't have any. None of my brothers or sisters had a large family like Mama and Papa. Harold and Ralph have one son; Willie Frank has two sons; Boyd has two daughters; Blanche has two boys and one girl; Charles has two girls and two boys, and Bruce has two girls and three boys.

We don't meet at Knox Place anymore. Ralph has moved and the house has been rented. I hope the renters appreciate what a wonderful old house it is. When we get together, it's usually at a park. The conversation always turns to what's happening in the world. Everyone is talking about Martin Luther King, Jr. and the civil rights march from Selma to Montgomery. Everybody said they would have taken part in the march if they had been there, all, that is, except Harold. He said he had enough of causes, and he still has problems with old war wounds when it rains. We didn't dare talk about the Vietnam War, which is still going on.

The next year, we got together and the topic was the doctor who did the first heart transplant. Someone thought it was a great breakthrough. Maybe a heart transplant would help Bruce and Charles who have serious heart problems. When Bruce was a boy, everybody took turns listening to his heart. When Mama took him to the clinic for a checkup, every doctor in the clinic would come in to listen to Bruce's heart; his heart sounded like a waterfall. Bruce's heart trouble sure kept him from getting a lot of well-deserved spankings. Charles got out of quite a few too, but he is the baby of the family.

Morgan said, "I don't like the idea of using some dead person's heart in your body."

"Why not, they don't need it anymore when they are dead?"

"It seems kind of disrespectful to me."

"When did you start thinking about what's respectable?"

"Well, Pru, I want you to know, when I kick off, I want all my parts to go with me."

"Don't worry, Morgan, I think your parts will be worn out."

The family had a good laugh. "Morgan isn't the only one who's worn out." Harold said.

1968

I can't believe it—Jackie Kennedy got married! She married a Greek shipping millionaire named Onassis. I can't imagine why she did that. She and John made such a lovely couple. Jackie and Onassis don't even look right together. People get lonely, I guess.

President Kennedy's brother, Robert, is running for President and has done well in the primaries. He will be here next week, speaking in a park about a mile away. Many of my friends and neighbors are going to listen to him. He is almost as good a speaker as President Kennedy was. It would be strange to have two President Kennedys. Maybe not, there were two Roosevelts.

I decided to watch Robert Kennedy on television. In the middle of the speech, Bobby Kennedy announced Martin Luther King. Jr. had been assassinated. I didn't hear the rest of his speech. Many who went to see

Bobby Kennedy in the park left in tears. Riots broke out around the country. Thankfully, there were none here in Indianapolis. A few months later, Bobby Kennedy was assassinated. How can the Kennedy family bare all this pain? I don't know if I could.

Richard Nixon has finally become our 37th President after several tries. To his credit, he has started to withdraw our troops from Vietnam. Maybe this is the beginning of the end of so much dying.

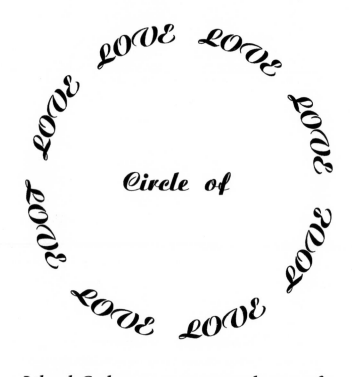

Circle of LOVE

I thank God upon every remembrance of you.

—*Philippians 1:3*

Circle of Love

◆

Morgan Jr. has four children, one boy and three girls. Phyllis has one girl. I enjoy my grandchildren so much. I'm amazed that time passes so quickly. It seems just a few years ago when my children were babies.

Morgan Sr. enjoys his grandchildren too. He spends most of his time at home now. His friends come to see him often, in spite of how he insults them by asking them to go home. They love being in his company.

Morgan has worked as a presser at a cleaners owned by a Greek family for several years. Like everyone else, they are very fond of him and put up with whatever he does. They have been concerned about him lately, and so have I. He hasn't been well and doesn't want to go to the doctor. He has been at home for the last few days, and keeps insisting he's feeling better. I'm not convinced.

Morgan spent the weekend calling his old Army buddies in Cincinnati and California. He seems different this week, kind, gentle and considerate, like he was when we first married. I remember when we married and I left my family, I was so lonely. I missed Mama, Papa and my sisters and brothers so much. They lived only a few blocks away but it wasn't the same. As much as I loved Morgan's mother, I always felt one woman in a house was quite enough.

Every evening, I would wait for him to come home. I would always ask him what he brought me. Sometimes he would have candy in his pocket, and would hold my arms down to keep me from searching his pockets for my gift. The early years were good. It has been years since Morgan told me he loved me. This week, he told me several times. I found that odd.

Morgan told me a few of his friends were coming to see him over the weekend. I asked him who, how many, and where were they staying. He said, "Don't worry about it." I did worry about it. Our home is too small for a lot of company. On Friday night, they came. Six of his loyal and devoted buddies, one was from California, one from Cincinnati, one from Kentucky, two from St. Louis, and one from Terre Haute, Indiana. I know the neighbors were probably curious about all the cars parked in front. Morgan and his friends talked about Army days and their families. They toasted everyone they could think of, and talked until they were exhausted. They slept in chairs, in the children's room, and on the floor. This went on from Friday until Sunday afternoon.

I have never seen such friendship. I found the whole thing absolutely appalling. I left home as much as possible. I am not going to empty another ashtray, or cook another meal. Having six men in the house is just too much. They are polite enough, but it is grating on my nerves. When the last one left on Sunday afternoon, I was exhausted and overjoyed. At last, I have my house back. I tried not to let Morgan know how disgusted I was about so much company. I know he missed his friends, but I have never understood why he has always wanted so many friends around him. A neighbor said he is gregarious. I agreed but I didn't know what the word meant. I must look it up.

The quiet is absolutely heavenly after spending the weekend listening to the sound of men's voices, one trying to "*out-lie*" the other. Morgan had a wonderful time. Perhaps now I can have my husband to myself for a while.

On Monday morning, Morgan didn't feel like going to work. That came as no surprise to me. He didn't seem to have his usual spark. Tuesday morning, he decided he needed to stay home one more day. I agreed that he should. I kissed him good-bye and left for work. Around 5:00 that evening, I got off the bus and walked the block and a half home. It is a beautiful October day. I love this time of year when leaves start to change colors, and it is warm during the day and cool at night. The only thing I don't like about it is that it precedes winter. I hate being cold. I spoke to the neighbors who were in their yards raking leaves. They all asked about Morgan.

I wonder what Morgan has been doing all day, watching television, no doubt. Sometimes I can hear him laughing at something on the television long before I reach the house. Today, I heard the television as I reached the porch. I went in and called to him. There was no answer. I looked around the house and in the back yard. He isn't here. Next to his favorite chair is a bottle of beer, still cold to the touch. A cigarette had burned to a long ash. I snuffed it out.

I heard Mrs. Amos calling me. Her voice sounded urgent. Mrs. Amos is the elderly lady who lives two doors away. She and her husband, Reverend Amos, have been our neighbors for years. I have spent many evenings, sitting on the Amos' swing on her front porch, listening to her stories and sage advice. The Amoses are a wonderful couple. They were the first in the neighborhood to own a car. It was a Model-T Ford with a running board.

When Mrs. Amos reached the house, she was out of breath. I couldn't understand what she was saying. I asked her to sit down. Both Reverend and Mrs. Amos are in their nineties. After a few minutes, Mrs. Amos was able to speak. She said her husband had fallen in the back yard and she couldn't get him up. She called Morgan and asked him to help her. He told her he would be right down.

"I'm glad he helped, Mrs. Amos. Is there anything I can do?"

"You had better come quick," she said, taking my hand.

As we walked, Mrs. Amos said Morgan lifted Reverend Amos up from the ground, took him inside and put him on the bed. Morgan said to her, "That wore me out." He sat in her big, overstuffed chair to rest.

I went in Mrs. Amos' house. When I saw Morgan, I knew. I could not say it; I could not believe it. I pulled up a chair next to him and tried to will him back to me. How could he do it? How could he leave me? I had had so little of his life. When I left him this morning, I asked him to promise me he would stay at home and rest and not have any of his friends over. He promised he would stay at home.

I called Phyllis. I don't remember what I told her. She lives ten minutes away. It seemed she arrived in just a few minutes. She said nothing but went to her Dad. She laid his head against her chest. I could see the tiny gold ring with diamond chips on the smallest finger of her right hand. Did she always wear it? I don't remember now. She had kept that tiny *circle of love* her father had so proudly given her over twenty-five years ago. She cradled his head and spoke to him softly, knowing he couldn't hear her now. I couldn't hear her words. Perhaps I wasn't supposed to. Oh, God, how she loved him!

I was unable to do anything. I had to leave all of the arrangements to my children. Rev. Amos' health improved. He was sorry he wasn't strong enough to attend the funeral. After the funeral, Phyllis stayed for the rest of the day. It is getting late, so I told her she should go home. I assured her I would be all right, but she slept on the davenport all night. I couldn't sleep. I have never been able to sleep when Morgan isn't at home. I guess I'll have to learn how. I just laid there and thought of all the people I love who have passed away.

Weeks have passed and I still can't sleep at night. I survive by falling asleep for short periods of time during the day. Every night, I say goodnight to Morgan's picture. It's the one in his Army uniform. He looks so handsome in that picture.

As usual, I can't sleep. I just lie here, praying and thinking. Everything is quiet. The house has stopped creaking and has settled in for the night. I look at the "Glow-in-the-Dark" clock. It's a little past midnight. I hear a sound like the rustling of clothes. There's a smell—it's like cigarettes and

Old Spice after shave. I hold my breath. I'm afraid to breathe. I am lying on my side, facing the clock. I can feel the bed on Morgan's side go down. I dare not turn over or speak. There's no need. I'm not going to fuss. I'm just glad he's home. I knew he would keep his promise.

Thank God he's home. Now I can sleep. Now, I can sleep...

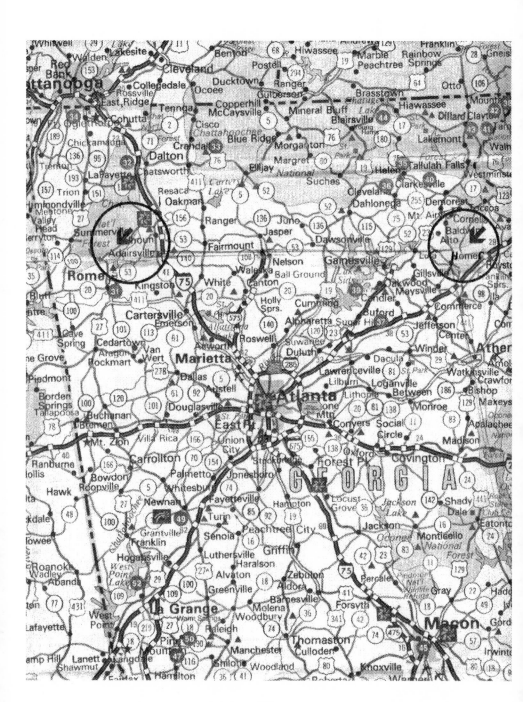

Epilogue

By the Side of the Road

It has been almost 30 years since my father, Morgan Adair, Sr., died. At times, I still find myself looking for him, and longing to see his bright smile and hear his cheerful voice. Mother, Prudence Adair, is now in a nursing home and still has fond memories of her home and childhood in Homer, Georgia. She was excited when I told her I was going to Homer, Georgia. I made a promise to myself many years ago that I would see Homer, Georgia.

A friend and I drove to Nashville, Tennessee, then to Pigeon Forge, Gatlinburg and to the breathtaking Smoky Mountains. The haze that hangs in the mountains is a spectacular sight. The height causes my ears to pop, and driving is slow because of the treacherous hairpin turns. As beautiful as it is, I breathe a sigh of relief as we leave the mountains and go through the County of Cherokee. We stop there for a while to rest.

Homer is not far away and my heart is beating so fast. I can hardly breathe. I try to drink in the surroundings because I don't feel I will ever return. Some tall pine trees are completely covered by Kudzu, the plant which covers everything in its path. The kudzu-covered trees look like giant green monsters from a science fiction movie. Beautiful fuchsia colored bushes, unlike any I have ever seen, adorn the roadside. The air is fresh and the sky appears bluer here. A green sign points out that we are close to Homer. Our rented car isn't moving fast enough. I can't wait to get there. I feel as if I have waited a lifetime for this moment. Most of my family and friends cannot understand why it is so important to me. I don't know if I can explain it.

There is little to see from the highway but I'm not surprised. I would have been disappointed if it had turned out to be a thriving metropolis. I wanted to see Homer as my mother saw it over 75 years ago, and I did. I see a few farms, a grocery store, a church and the Chamber of Commerce. Directly behind the Chamber of Commerce is the courthouse. Across the street, built 100 years ago, is the jail. It is an historic landmark, presently used as a tourist attraction. I read it still has a hanging trap for executions. We pull up to the City-County building and park. I sit there silently. My friend breaks the silence by asking, "How do you feel?" I can't reply for a moment. It took a great deal of effort to answer. I say hoarsely, "I don't know." I really do but I am ashamed to tell her. I am excited, grateful and terrified. It took a great deal of effort to keep from shaking. I don't know why. We enter the City-County building and I ask where I can inquire about birth certificates.

I find the right department and ask the clerk if there are records of births of the Knoxes. I want to find out if there might be a record of my grandfather's birth. I don't think it is possible, but I want to be sure. My grandfather was born April 6, 1872. The clerk tells me they didn't keep birth certificates back then. She is too polite to say they didn't keep birth records for people of color back then. She is able to locate records of some of the Knox children's births. Mother had told me the children who were delivered by midwives had no birth certificates. Those few who were delivered by doctors did. This proved to be true. I try to find birth certificates for my grandmothers with no success. I thank the clerk for her help and turn to leave.

"Where y'all from," she asks.

"Indianapolis, Indiana," I reply.

"That's a long ways away," she says.

"A very long ways," I mumble.

"Are you terribly disappointed about not finding the birth certificates?" my friend asks.

"No, that really wasn't what I came for; I wanted to see this town and to walk where my mother might have walked," I say

with a lump in my throat.

As we walk to the car, we almost bump into three unkempt white teenagers who have no intention of giving up any space on the sidewalk. They are wearing cutoffs, unlaced tennis shoes and gray T-shirts with a confederate flag on them. I smile at them; they stare and give us a look of curiosity. I don't believe Homer has many African-American visitors.

My friend asks if I would like to go to the library to talk to the librarian I had spoken to by phone a few weeks ago. "Yes, I would," I said. I take a few pictures of the courthouse and jail then proceed to find the library. We stop at the grocery to ask directions to the library. As we start to leave, I see an elderly black man sitting in a red truck. He is smiling and waving. I ask my friend to stop the car because I want to talk to him. I walk over to the truck and say, "Good afternoon, Sir. How are you today?"

He smiles and I can see the deep wrinkles in his face; and there are several teeth missing. He has a tube running from his nose to an oxygen tank which lays on the seat beside him. He tips his cap and says, "Ma'am, you don't want to hear 'bout everything that's wrong with me, but I guess I'm pretty good considerin'. Y'all visitin' down here?"

I wonder how he knew. He can't see our out-of-town plates from where he sits. He probably knows everyone in town. I think he sat in his truck by the side of the road because he had nothing better to do. I tell the man my family was born in Homer and we are from Indiana. I ask him if he knows any Knoxes. He scratches his forehead and says, "I'm 71 years old and I've been here all my life." (He looked much older.) He said he didn't know any Knoxes but he was sure there were some people in Homer who probably would. I ask him if he knows where Kings Branch cemetery is. He says, "I've been there more times than I have fingers and toes, but I can't 'member rightly where it is." Kings Branch cemetery is where mother's grandmother and infant sister were buried. The old gentleman is pleasant and I can sense he wants to talk more; so, I ask him directions back to the main highway. He is able to give clear directions. I thank him and turn to leave, hating to do so. For some reason, I feel a kind of kinship to this man and it soothes the unexplained fear I feel. Before I can get back into the car, the old man shouts, "You take care now, be real careful and watch them trucks!" I wave to him and leave to find the library. Why didn't I ask his name?

We drive down the road toward the library. I begin to feel uneasy. When I mention this to my friend, I am surprised she has the same feeling. We abort the idea of the library. She drives slowly to allow me to see as much of Homer as I can. My uneasy feeling is probably contagious. There probably is nothing to fear. I just can't forget that my mother and family left this town they loved because of the Ku Klux Klan. I certainly feel no acrimony, only relief and gratitude that they were able to leave unharmed. I know it could not have been done without help.

I now know more about that small dot on the Georgia map called Homer, Georgia (Banks County) than I ever thought possible. It is only 62 miles North of Atlanta. Interstate 85 provides a link, not only to Atlanta, but to Greenville, Spartanburg and Charlotte. Homer is the county seat. Eight miles away, at Banks Crossing, there are motels, restaurants and a shopping center with over 100 outlet stores. According to Guinness World Book of Records, Homer hosts the world's largest Easter egg hunt. It attracts tourists from as far away as Pennsylvania. What an odd claim to fame. The other Homer claim to fame is that it's the birthplace of Hall of Fame baseball player, Ty Cobb.

The Chamber of Commerce was built in 1859 with slave labor. The Chamber is working hard to attract families who are trying to get away from larger cities. There is a bit of confusion about the population. The librarian said it is 200. The Chamber of Commerce said 741 in one publication, and 11,388 in another. It all depends on whom you talk to.

To those passing through, Homer may be just a few buildings by the side of the road, but it was home to my family. I will always be grateful to have seen this place and to those responsible for helping my family to leave it.

A few days later, we arrive back home. The following day, I decide to see the Knoxes first Indianapolis home.

I drive to an area of Indianapolis called Brightwood to see if I can find The Knoxes first Indianapolis home. I have passed the street many times. Mother still remembers the address. I expect to find a vacant lot or an old boarded up house. Not so; it is as Mother described, down to the cement banisters and the tree in front. There is white aluminum siding on the house, and a small lot on each side. The lawn is well kept. I circle the block and can see that at one time it had been a lovely neighborhood. I park the car in front of the old homestead. Thoughts fill my mind about my 90-year-old mother. Her steps are slow, she walks with a walker, and her hearing isn't what it used to be. Her mind is sharp, and behind her twinkling bespectacled eyes, I can see the ten-year-old stepping from that porch in her homemade dress, with ribboned hair, on her way to school. Homesick, scared and excited.

I think, if I should live to say a last good-bye to Mother, and I must release her hand, God, please take it, then let her spirit run free, past the fence covered with honeysuckle, the peach trees, the creek and through the beautiful woods of Homer, Georgia (Banks County) one last time!

Notes

"A deeply touching saga of one family's experience flowing richly across three generations. Wind Chimes and Promises is dramatic, suspenseful, funny. Most of all human. It tugs heartstrings and beckons the imagination through the specter of human emotions. Everyone in America is talking about race. Phyllis Adair's work enhances the discussion."

—**James Patterson**, Editorial Writer
The Indianapolis Star

"Phyllis Adair's flowing style and her fascinating material provide a riveting experience. Begin in 1919 with the exciting flight from Homer, Georgia of Will and Sally Knox and their ten children, assisted by the mysterious Miss Abigail. Follow the Indianapolis fortunes of the Knox and Adair families through the next fifty years as seen from the viewpoint of the author's mother, Prudence Knox Adair. You'll enjoy it all."

— **Laura Gaus**
Teacher, Author

"A mother's love for her daughter and a daughter's love for her mother candidly couched in a carefully crafted and powerful slice of African-American history. Profoundly simple and simply profound."

                                —Bishop T. Garrott Benjamin, Jr.
                                           Senior Pastor, Light of the World
                                        Christian Church; Indianapolis, IN.